The kingdom of heaven is one of the most talked about concepts of Jesus' ministry, and at the same time, the most misunderstood. Robby helps the reader understand Jesus' focus on the here and now and not just the there and then of the kingdom. After reading this book, you will be motivated to live on mission to make disciples of all nations.

Ed Stetzer, Billy Graham Distinguished Chair
Wheaton College

It's hard to keep Jesus' command to seek first the kingdom of God when so many Christians seem not to have a clue what the kingdom is. Robby Gallaty is one of the nation's most dynamic and revered pastors. In this book, he conducts an accessible investigation into the kingdom, and our lives in it. You may not agree with every single one of his conclusions, but, whether you do or not, the questions provoked will help you to pray, and to live, the way Jesus taught us to do.

Russell Moore, president, Ethics and Religious Liberty Commission of the Southern Baptist Convention and best-selling author of *Onward* and *The Storm-Tossed Family*

Robby helps us move from an incomplete, two-chapter gospel (fall, redemption) to the full four-chapter gospel of the kingdom: creation, fall, redemption, restoration. He helps us understand that our lives and world come from the kingdom and are headed toward the kingdom of God *on earth as it is in heaven*. In other words, those of us who claim to be Jesus-followers are to live *here and now* as viral kingdom agents. Robby's combination of scholarly reflection and profound insight is nothing less than inspiring!

Reggie McNeal, author of *Kingdom Come*

ors

D0830559

It is rare when a respected friend writes something you like so much that you think, *I could have written that!* The famous theologian Karl Barth commented on the first chapter of Dietrich Bonhoeffer's classic book, *The Cost of Discipleship*. He said that it was so good that he wouldn't attempt to edit it, he would just copy it word for word. That is the way I feel about Robby's introduction and comments on the need for a more robust gospel that includes discipleship as natural part of what it means to be saved. Gallaty's work is getting deeper and deeper.

Bill Hull, author of *The Disciple Making Pastor, Conversion and Discipleship, The Christian Leader,* and *The Discipleship Gospel,* and cofounder of the Bonhoeffer Project

I applaud Gallaty for seeking to ground his view of the kingdom in a historically informed, critically aware reading of Scripture. The result is a message that is neither shallow nor dry, directed toward the serious Bible reader but not written in overly technical language. Gallaty challenges nonscholars but doesn't overwhelm them. More importantly, Gallaty writes as a pastor who is conversant with the top scholarship in this area but who is also in tune with the thought of his congregation. I heartily recommend this book.

Robert B. Stewart, professor of Philosophy and Theology, Greer-Heard Chair of Faith and Culture, New Orleans Baptist Theological Seminary

This book is the marriage of Robby's commitment to discipleship and his passion for the kingdom of our King. The result is an insightful and challenging read about life for the believer in the here and the now.

Eric Geiger, senior pastor, Mariners Church

HERE AND NOW

HERE

THRIVING IN THE

AND

KINGDOM OF HEAVEN TODAY

NOW

ROBBY GALLATY

PUBLISHING GROUP

NASHVILLE, TENNESSEE

978-1-4627-5786-2

Published by B&H Publishing Group
Nashville, Tennessee

Dewey Decimal Classification: 248.84
Subject Heading: CHRISTIAN LIFE \ HAPPINESS \ HEAVEN

Cover design by Jared Callais.
Author photo © Joanna McVey.

Any italics found in Scripture references
has been placed there by author for emphasis.

1 2 3 4 5 6 7 • 22 21 20 19

To Bryant and Anne Wright

You have exemplified the principles in this book over the years Kandi and I have known you. Your passion for Christ is contagious and evident to everyone who knows you. I'm eternally grateful for your investment in my life.

ACKNOWLEDGMENTS

A s with any writing project, the contents inside are the result of years of research and study. I first began thinking about the kingdom of heaven as a present reality after listening to Dwight Pryor speak about it in his Kingdom Unveiled DVD series. Since then, I've listened to literally every teaching his ministry has made available at jcstudies.org.

Others who have impacted my understanding of this concept are Arnold Fruchtenbaum, D. T. Lancaster, Ray Vander Laan, Lois Tverberg, Marvin Wilson, James Whitman, and Boaz Michael. The insights I gleaned over the years shaped the development and direction of this work.

Scot McKnight, Reggie McNeal, Ryan Lambert, and Bill Hull helped me think pastorally about how we live in the kingdom of heaven today. Each of their books offered practical steps we can take to not only to live but thrive in it.

I also want to thank Hamilton Barber, Chris Swain, Taylor Combs, Chuck Quarles, Russell Moore, and Devin Maddox for critical feedback to strengthen the work. This book would not be what it is without your assistance.

As with every book I've written, I could not have completed it without the help of my wife, Kandi. She is my greatest sounding board for ideas, illustrations, and insights to strengthen the arguments this book presents.

CONTENTS

PREFACE

As with any book that encourages the reader to rethink a familiar concept, it's important to establish the purpose of this work. The kingdom of heaven has been a concept discussed, debated, and preached on since the conception of the nation of Israel. Instead of trying to interpret what the concept means today, we must uncover what it meant to the ancient audience to which it was spoken.

My passion for many years has been to place Jesus back into the context in which He lived. Unlike the popular opinion of some today, He's not a blonde haired, blue-eyed American pastor. He was a dark-skinned, middle-eastern Rabbi. As a result, many implications can arise from our misunderstanding of Jesus and His ministry, one of which is our view of the kingdom of heaven.

Throughout this work, I will attempt to change your perspective from a futuristic mind-set of the kingdom only to a present reality of God's power today. The kingdom has two aspects working simultaneously: already/not yet. While Jesus inaugurated the kingdom of heaven with His first coming, we will not realize the fullness of the kingdom until His second coming. My goal with this work is to swing the pendulum back from an "under-realized eschatology," only future, to a more balanced understanding of the "both/and" nature of the eastern culture. Even though we will not experience every aspect of the kingdom until Jesus returns, we are invited to enter into and experience, in part, the kingdom here and now.

Join me as we embark on a journey to join God in the work H e is already engaged in today!

INTRODUCTION

Thoughts of Heaven

Imagine me, a six-foot-six, two hundred-and-eighty-five-pound twenty-six-year-old sitting in a practice room with my music teacher, preparing "I Can Only Imagine" for an upcoming music recital. See, I'd taken the hint. Weeks of people in my church secretively turning their heads to locate whoever it was making that awful racket during worship.

I couldn't help it. I love singing Christian songs. I love the refrains that reflect on lives well lived and the future glory of heaven. For those who don't know my story, God saved me as a twenty-six-year-old out of a life of drug and alcohol addiction. I'd never sung a Christian song prior to that time. Therefore, I found myself singing about "Beulah Land," or exclaiming that "I'll Fly Away" "When the Roll Is Called Up Yonder," because "This World Is Not My Home." I couldn't wait to see the "Mansion on a Hilltop" that waits for me on the other side of eternity.

Much of the way the gospel has been packaged in modern times revolves around this sort of language—joining up with God's kingdom after we die. If you think about it, even our prayers, our services, our creeds, our liturgies, and our motivation is geared toward tomorrow. If you boil the Christian life down for many, the ultimate hope of believers is to get to heaven, essentially leave this world, after you die. It seems that our obsession with the future causes us to care little about what God is doing today.

Think of the last time you heard a sermon about the kingdom of heaven. Better yet, think of the last conversation you discussed the kingdom of heaven. If you're like most Christians, you may not have an answer. Sadly, most rarely think about the kingdom, much less speak about it. This, however, was not the case for Jesus. For Him, the kingdom of heaven was the predominate topic of His ministry. His message about the kingdom was more than a reminder to obtain your ticket to the great Disney World in the Sky—something it would seem many Christians are hoping and waiting for.

Is our obsession with leaving this world and transporting to heaven the same message Jesus taught on the kingdom in the Gospels? Are we talking about the same concept? I believe we may have a kingdom conundrum on our hands and don't know it.

Let's answer a simpler question first: *Why did Jesus come to Earth?* You might respond, "To show people how to avoid hell and enter heaven." While this was a subset of His earthly agenda, we undervalue the thrust of Jesus' ministry message when we focus on the future at the expense of the present. When Jesus speaks of the kingdom of heaven in the Gospels, He envisioned God's kingdom rule and reign in the present day on Earth, not just a day when believers would be ejected into the spiritual realm. Sadly, this misunderstanding has plagued and paralyzed believers from experiencing the "abundant life" that Jesus promised (John 10:10).

Born for Today, Not Just Tomorrow

By focusing on one aspect of our salvation, we, whether knowingly or unknowingly, minimize other aspects of our Christian life. If justification is the entirety of our salvation experience, believers miss out on the joy and purpose of sanctification. Dallas Willard summarizes it this way:

> The background assumption is that justification is the entirety of salvation. If you are justified— your sins forgiven—then you are saved and you will be "okay" after your death. I submit to you that this is what is offered, in still more specific forms, by current efforts ("evangelism") to convert people to Christianity, and it is what people generally understand to be essential to the transaction.[1]

If the purpose of Christianity is just to enter heaven, Jesus wouldn't have left us on Earth after He saved us. We'd be raptured without a second to spare to enjoy eternity with Him. Surely the purpose of the kingdom of heaven is greater than just achieving eternal life.

In fact, our obsession with getting to heaven could be paralyzing, even problematic. I heard someone say once, "When you're so heavenly minded, you can become no earthly good." When believers are self-absorbed, only focused on their own eternal rewards in heaven, we lose sight of our calling on Earth. Jesus gave us a commission to make reproducible followers of Him. It's called the Great Co-Mission for a reason: God expects our involvement. The reason He didn't eject us into the elysian fields of paradise the moment we were born again is because there's work to be done. You were saved not just from the world, but for the world.

Most evangelistic tactics move people toward making a decision or a convert; however, Jesus and His disciples focused on making disciples. New birth is necessary to move from life to death, but it doesn't end there. Derwin Gray, pastor of Transformation Church, told me in a phone conversation, "The apostle Paul wouldn't understand the invitations issued at the conclusion of many services today." "Raise a hand," "walk an aisle," "say a prayer," and "repeat after me" are foreign concepts to the apostle. I'm not necessarily arguing for or against any of these methods. My point is that they should not be an end in themselves, but a means to introducing people to a life of discipleship.

Sadly, we have reduced salvation to a transaction where if sinners provide the correct answers to a mental, spiritual questionnaire and say "Amen" at the right spots, we pronounce they are saved with nothing else required of them. Whether they follow Jesus after saying this prayer is optional. Whether they enjoy the blessings of the kingdom is up to them. Whether they replicate their lives into the lives of others is a choice, and the choice is typically no.

We've failed to see that salvation in Christ starts from a confession to follow Jesus, but it doesn't end there. Jesus expects so much more; He commands so much more.

In this model, *spiritual disciplines in the Christian life become recommended but not required activities.* Obedience is optional, reading the Bible is optional, and memorizing Scripture is optional. Praying and fasting are optional as well. Whether I share the gospel with a lost person is merely a choice I make. Surely this can't be what Jesus envisioned when He commanded His followers to "make disciples of all nations"?

Surprisingly, moving people through a process from making a decision to becoming a maturing follower of Jesus is foreign in many churches today. An escapism mentality, on the other hand, permeates our evangelistic conversations: "You don't want to go to hell, do you? It's hot down there. Choose heaven so you can spend eternity with God." While this is true, is it the whole gospel?

For many years, we have preached half the gospel by encouraging people to be saved FROM something—namely sin, wrath, damnation, and eternal punishment—and neglected the fact that we're saved FOR something. Student ministries in churches across America will serve as an example. Typical youth pastors navigate students through the three-humped camel: disciple now or D-Now (which should be called E-Now because it leans toward being a one-time evangelistic event), summer camp, and fall retreat. Each of these is formative in the life of a student; however, the goal is to see lost people saved while believers hear sermons about going to a place they are already heading to. And we wonder why two-thirds of our students never come back to church after going off to college![2]

Scot McKnight in his book, *The King Jesus Gospel*, stresses that by "focusing youth events, retreats, and programs on persuading people to make a decision disarms the gospel, distorts the numbers, and diminishes the significance of discipleship."[3] If we gauge our success by catching the lost only, we will overlook the saved. Rather than focusing on one over the other, I would submit we adopt a both/and mind-set.

According to Barna Research, half of all Christians who make a decision to follow Jesus do so before the age of thirteen, while two-thirds accept Christ before they turn eighteen.[4] If we perpetuate the "three-humped camel" approach, the majority of our ministry efforts will be directed toward the few lost people in the room. They will mostly hear evangelistic messages about avoiding hell and obtaining heaven. Six camp sermons a year for seven years (sixth–twelfth grade), forty-two messages to be exact, that didn't equip them to share their faith, to grow as a Christian, to defend what they believe, or to endure hardship when life gets tough. No wonder they don't know why they believe what they believe. No wonder they are unable to provide a defense for the hope that is within them.

The Good News

One of the problems is our understanding of the word *gospel*. It has pivoted from a "disciplistic" emphasis in Jesus' day to a "decisionistic" personal salvation event in ours. We now reduce the gospel to getting our sins forgiven so we go to heaven after we die. This explains why so few churches have a systematic process for discipling their people. What's the point? We're all going to heaven at the end, right?

Even the creeds we hold to as believers advance from Jesus' birth to death without a mention of His life. Take the Apostles' Creed, written in AD 390, for example:

> I believe in God, the Father Almighty, maker of heaven and earth; And in Jesus Christ his only Son, our Lord; who was conceived by the Holy Spirit, born of the Virgin Mary, suffered under Pontius Pilate, was crucified, dead, and buried; the third day he rose from the dead; he ascended into heaven, and sitteth at the right hand of God the Father Almighty; from thence he shall come to judge the quick and the dead. I believe in the

Holy Spirit, the holy catholic church, the com-
munion of saints, the forgiveness of sins, the
resurrection of the body, and the life everlasting.
Amen.[5]

Nothing is mentioned after Jesus' birth about His life other
than His suffering under Pilate. Similarly, the Nicene Creed
(AD 325) gives a nod to Jesus' life with the phrase "and became
man," but implies Christ's kingdom will launch at His second
coming: "He will come again in glory to judge the living and the
dead, and his kingdom will have no end."[6]

Now, this is not to say the creeds are unimportant in the
history of the church. Many men put their lives and their credi-
bility on the line to contend for the central truths of the gospel.
Moreover, the creeds were usually reactionary—responding to
various heresies that arose in the early church—so they addressed
specific doctrines, and not every prevailing issue of the times.

Because of this, the creeds can inadvertently contribute to
the mistaken belief of many that Jesus' life was less important
than His death. New Testament theologian N. T. Wright challenges those who gloss over Jesus' life by asking: "What is the
point, I have asked, of the healing and feastings, the Sermon on
the Mount and the controversies with the Pharisees, the stilling
of the storm, Peter's confession at Caesarea Philippi, and so on,
and so on."[7] Jesus' earthly ministry prepared the disciples, and
us, for future ministry.

Growing up as Catholic, I learned and recited the Lord's
Prayer regularly. The assumption in praying those words was that
by doing so, Christ would return one future day to instate His
kingdom. As we will learn, this prayer, in contrast to what we've
been taught, promises a *present* kingdom for those who obey the
King today, not just a gold-paved one tomorrow.

But what are we to do, then, with the promise of eternal life? John 3:16 ends with this promise: "For God loved the world in this way: He gave his one and only Son, so that everyone who believes in him will not perish but have *eternal life*." Some translations have "everlasting life" in place of eternal life, but the confusion still remains. What we will find is that when the rich young ruler asks, "What must I do to inherit *eternal life*?" he isn't inquiring about what words to pray in order to secure a spot in heaven. He wants to know how to experience heaven on Earth. The Kingdom New Testament translates this verse, "Good teacher, what must I do to inherit the life of the age to come" (Luke 18:18).[8] Interestingly, Jesus doesn't respond like many pastors today would by telling him to repeat a prayer in order to get saved. In fact, Jesus never mentions faith, trust, belief or repentance. He tells him to do something: "Sell everything you have and give it to the poor and then follow me." We'll unpack this concept in chapter six.

Where Is Heaven?

As we begin to get a full view of heaven, let's look for a moment at what Paul wrote regarding the heavenly realm in 2 Corinthians 12:2–3: "I know a man in Christ who was caught up to the *third heaven* fourteen years ago. Whether he was in the body or out of the body, I don't know; God knows. I know that this man—whether in the body or out of the body I don't know; God knows." This verse contains a phrase we're not entirely familiar with today.

In Paul's day, the Jews understood heaven in three categories (see Gen. 6:7, Deut. 4:19, and 2 Cor. 12:10 respectively). The first heaven was the atmosphere in which we live today. Humans, animals, and sea creatures inhabit this realm. The second heaven was outer space where planets and stars reside. The third heaven was the dwelling place of God, at times given the designation "paradise." We see this in Luke 23:43, "And he said to him, 'Truly I tell you, today you will be with me in paradise,'" and in Revelation 2:7, "Let anyone who has ears to hear listen to what the Spirit says to the churches. To the one who conquers, I will give the right to eat from the tree of life, which is in the paradise of God."

Heaven is not a future destination hidden in the solar system; it's the supernatural dimension of God. But in the verses from 2 Corinthians, Paul connected the two worlds together. The spiritual and the physical meeting in one place. In his case, he experienced it in the present.

First-century residents of Israel would have understood the immediacy of God's kingdom on Earth. Wright explains the mind-set of the early Christians:

> When Jesus tells the brigand [thief on the cross] that he will join him in paradise that very day, paradise clearly cannot be their ultimate destination, as Luke's next chapter makes clear. Paradise is, rather, the blissful garden where God's people rest prior to the resurrection. When Jesus declares that there are many dwelling places in his father's house, the word for dwelling place is *mone,* which denotes a temporary lodging. When Paul says that his desire is "to depart to be with Christ which is far better," he is indeed shining of a blissful life with his Lord immediately after death, but this is only the prelude to the resurrection itself.[9]

The prevailing mind-set of a first-century believer was a renewed vocation on Earth, not a spot in heaven. *Today, most Christians are trying to get out of this world; Jesus desires to break into this world through them.* His is not a salvation "out of" the world; it is a rescue mission "within" the world.[10]

What if the Christian life was so much more than just a one-time decision to secure a place in heaven? What if our absorption with having our names called on the heavenly roll has perpetuated missed opportunities in ministry here and now? What if you could experience heaven on Earth today? I'm not promising flying angels singing praise music as we enjoy our renewed, resurrected bodies. What I'm envisioning is the satisfied, abundant life Jesus promised. A life that—regardless of your circumstances or your present context—experiences joy, happiness, and peace that is difficult to encapsulate in human terms. What if heaven was available to us today?

I think it is.

Jesus spoke about God's kingdom more than any other topic. No other concept is even close. In *Here and Now*, we will journey together to uncover the nucleus of Jesus' message, which promises both a present and future reality for all who respond to the invitation to follow Him.

I will not devote much time explaining the nature of salvation, which is through faith alone, by grace alone, and in Christ alone. (For more information on the topic, I recommend Greg Gilbert's book *What Is the Gospel?* and Bruce Demarest's work *The Cross and Salvation.*) We don't work for our salvation: "For you are saved by grace through faith, and this is not from yourselves; it is God's gift—not from works, so that no one can boast" (Eph. 2:8–9). However, good works for the Lord will necessarily proceed from our salvation: "For we are his workmanship, created in Christ Jesus for good works, which God prepared ahead of time for us to do" (Eph. 2:10).

Also, I'm not arguing for or against a particular eschatological system, whether premillennialism, postmillennialism, or amillennialism. Scholars before me have written extensively on this topic. My concern is simply what is expected of Christ followers after they are born again until the time of death or until Christ's return, whichever comes first.

We will ask and answer the question: Now that we are saved *from* sin, what are we actually saved *for*?

SECTION 1

The King Among His People

CHAPTER 1

Good News for Today

Time Together

Driving up the mountain in Montreat, North Carolina, to spend the day with Billy Graham was an experience I will never forget. During my seminary studies, I had the privilege of listening to and examining many of his messages in the writing of my dissertation. To say I was excited was an understatement. Dr. Don Wilton, Graham's pastor, led his son Rob and I into his old log cabin home. After some introductions, we read Scripture out loud as Dr. Graham sat and listened. Reading Acts 2 on the revival of the early church to the man who gave his life to witnessing the world revived for Christ is humbling.

I was asked to share my testimony of God's grace in saving me from a life of alcohol abuse and addiction. Dr. Graham's response was "Praise the Lord!" Before departing, each of us took turns praying for him. As we drove down the mountain, I cherished the time we spent hanging out with a living hero of the faith. Since then, I've thought about that day often, but as impactful as it was, it fades in comparison to a single day in the presence of the Lord. The psalmist declared, "Better a day in your courts than a thousand elsewhere" (Ps. 84:10 NIV). Imagine the eternal bliss of being enveloped in the presence of God. The good news, according to Scripture, is that believers don't have to wait to dwell with God.

In fact, the Bible is bookended with images of God dwelling among His people. Genesis begins with it, and Revelation ends with it. The Torah—the first five books of the Bible—devotes two chapters to the account of God's creation of the world, but it allocates thirty describing the construction of the tabernacle, the duties of the priesthood, the rituals, and their meanings (thirteen in Exodus, thirteen in Leviticus, two in Numbers, and two in Deuteronomy). Years after entering the promised land, God gives Solomon specific instructions to construct a permanent structure, the Temple on Mount Moriah, so that He could dwell in the midst of His people permanently. In essence, God's creation of the universe was miraculous, but His desire to live among us is *paramount.*

God's design for heaven and Earth in Genesis points to the concept of a temple, a dwelling place for God. God then populated His Temple with people, fashioning mankind as an image of His glory. But sin marred that image; therefore, God took matters in His own hands by sending His Son to dwell as a man in order to accomplish the task Adam was incapable of doing— that is, living in perfect harmony with God. "What God does in sending the Son," says one theologian, "is to establish Jesus as the Messiah, which means King, and God established in Jesus Christ the kingdom of God, which means the King is ruling in His kingdom."[11] God "with us" is spoken of throughout the Bible (see Gen. 5:22; 21:14–22; 28:11–21; 39:3, 21–23; Exod. 4:1–15;

1 Sam. 18:12–16; 2 Chron. 15:2, 15; Ezra 8:22, 31; Pss. 37 and 121; Matt. 28:20; John 14:16–17; and Heb. 13:5–6).

The tabernacle in the Old Testament, and later the Temple, was a visible reminder of the transcendent, eternal God who had come to live with His people, and it was a sight to behold. The Sages of Israel used to say of the Second Temple (the Temple during the time of Jesus), "One who did not see the Temple in its constructed state, never saw a magnificent structure" (B. Sukkah 51b).[12] But even a finite structure was not the final resting place of God among His people.

When He created the Universe, the King of kings did so with a Word. John tells us that this Word created all things, came into the world, wrapped himself in flesh, and took up residence (tabernacled) among us (John 1:3, 14). God's kingdom came to Earth in the form of His Son, Jesus. While God brought His kingdom in the form of a temple in the Old Testament, the New Testament shows us that His kingdom came to Earth in the form of a *living* Temple, His Son, Jesus Christ. And what was the most talked about concept of Jesus' ministry? The kingdom of heaven.

What Is the Kingdom of Heaven?

The first time I heard the statement I'm about to share with you, it caught me completely off guard. As a result, it changed the way I viewed Jesus' ministry. Here's the statement: Jesus borrowed concepts and terms from the Jewish Sages, later called Rabbis, of His day.

The kingdom of heaven was a well-known concept spoken of by the Sages and the later Rabbis of Israel. When Jewish people recite the Shema (Deut. 6:4–9) twice daily, they are committing to take on the yoke of the kingdom by following God. By

repeating these words—"Listen, Israel: The LORD our God, the
LORD is one' Love the LORD your God with all your heart, with
all your soul, and with all your strength. These words that I am
giving you today are to be in your heart. Repeat them to your
children. Talk about them when you sit in your house and when
you walk along the road, when you lie down and when you get
up. Bind them as a sign on your hand and let them be a symbol
on your forehead.' Write them on the doorposts of your house
and on your city gates" (Deut. 6:4–9). Jews were taking on the
yoke of the kingdom. Not in some distant future, but right then,
in that moment, and every moment thereafter.

In the New Testament, Jesus personalizes the concept by
attaching it to God's authority over a person's responsibility to
accept or commit to aligning his life with God's will after salvation, as seen in John 14:23: "If anyone loves me, he will keep
my word. My Father will love him, and we will come to him
and make our home with him." For Jesus, it becomes a moral
obligation to obey the Lord. It's not a political overhaul, as some
thought in His day, namely John the Baptist, where God destroys
Israel's enemies and restores justice. The kingdom of heaven is
the work of God in the world today through kingdom citizens.
It's not just a realm to enter but also a ruling of God over our
present life.

A Hebraic Perspective

The first-century Hebrew understood the kingdom to be the
era of universal peace for God's chosen people. It's the messianic
reign promised specifically in Isaiah 11, Jeremiah 31, and Ezekiel
36. At this time, the throne will be restored to Israel through
the Messiah, God's anointed son of David, and the people will

enjoy prosperity, peace, and protection forever and ever as God removes their sins as far as the East is from the West. A new covenant will be formed with the people as God places His spirit within them by writing His law upon each of their hearts. Christ will reign over the Earth and every one of His followers will seek His kingdom first.[13]

When Jesus came to Earth, He extended this offer to us today. We can find the peace of our Messiah and enjoy aspects of His kingdom today. Think about it: It would not be good news if we had to wait for the kingdom to be set up, for we are still waiting after two thousand years for Jesus' second coming. Jesus consistently emphasized the present immediacy of God's power to heal, save, and redeem mankind. The kingdom has arrived in the person of Jesus and the power of Holy Spirit and is available to all who walk by the Spirit. We could say that Jesus is breaking into the present world today. If that's the case, we should quit asking to get out of it.

CHAPTER 2

A Wedding in the Wilderness

Have you ever walked in on someone midway through telling a story? Certain details that are pertinent to understanding the point of the story are missed. Paul Harvey made a career telling "the rest of the story" to his radio listeners. In 1976, Harvey provided hearers with forgotten insights or little known facts on a variety of topics with one key element, usually the name of an individual, kept to the end of the broadcast. He always concluded with the words, "And now you know the rest of the story."

Most Christians read the Bible in a similar way, spending time in the New Testament at the expense of the Old Testament. By only reading a quarter of the book, we miss the "rest of the story." We can't truly appreciate the New Testament without an understanding of the Old Testament.

Our preoccupation with part of the Bible—and our neglect of the other part—is brought to light in our gospel presentations. The history of the nation of Israel is all but removed from our evangelistic conversations. By doing this, we eliminate three-fourths of our modern Bibles. I have been guilty in years past of this oversight as well.

At one time, my gospel presentations started with creation in Genesis 1, moved to the fall in Genesis 3, and made a beeline to the New Testament with the birth of Christ. But what about the punishment for sins running rampant among mankind in Noah's day in Genesis 7, the expulsion of the nations for building a tower in Babylon to be like God, the call of and covenant with Abraham to make him the father of the nation of Israel (this is God's response to Adam's sin), the messiah-like figure Moses whom God used to liberate the people from the bondage of Egypt, the giving of the law and festivals as a foreshadowing of the Messiah (what Moses was incapable of doing by bringing the people into the promised land, the Messiah will do), Joshua's campaign to claim the promised land, the building of the Temple as a reminder of God's promise to dwell among His people, the Babylonian captivity as judgment for the rebellion of the nations, the prophets who warned and encouraged the people to turn back to God, and the silence after Malachi for four hundred years setting the stage for John the Baptist crying in the wilderness as the Elijah-like figure promised from the days of old? If none of this is pertinent for salvation, why devote three-fourths of the Bible to recording its history?

I'm not suggesting that every gospel presentation must walk the hearer through the entire meta-narrative of Scripture, for many times we only have a short time to explain the gospel. However, we should understand how God brought His people out of captivity so He could be with them. Biblical scholars B. T. Arnold and B. E. Beyer wrote, "The purpose for the exodus from Egypt was so God could *dwell* in the midst of His people. The coming of God's glorious presence into the newly constructed tabernacle forms the climax of the book of Exodus (40:34)."[14] By glossing over the Old Testament, we miss the picture of how God redeems in order to rule and reign over His people.

A King Is Reigning

When you explore a biblical concept, it is standard practice to examine the first instance of the concept you are studying. Where are biblical readers first introduced to God reigning as a king? You may think of the dynasty of King David or his son Solomon. Others may call to mind the rebuilding of the Temple in Nehemiah's day. Neither of these answers are correct. As noted already, the kingdom of God is not a locale we enter into, but rather God working among His people. In reality, the first mention of God's kingdom in the Bible is in the context of the exodus from Egypt. The people have just been set free from captivity through God's miraculous works.

God directed Moses to approach Pharaoh with a request to let His people go. Over the course of ten plagues, God displays His power over the gods and goddesses of Egypt:

> The plague of blood defeated Khnum, the River god of the Nile.
>
> The plague of frogs defeated Heket, the frog goddess of Egypt.
>
> The plague of lice defeated Aker, the earth god of Egypt.
>
> The plague of flies defeated Khepri, the fly god of Egypt.
>
> The plague on the cattle defeated Hathor/Ptah, the Egyptian goddesses associated with bulls and cows.

The plague of boils defeated Imhotep, the healing god of Egypt.

The plague of hail defeated Nut, the Egyptian sky god.

The plague of locusts defeated Renenutet, the field god of the harvest.

The plague of darkness defeated Ra, the Egyptian sun god.

The tenth plague was the most devastating attack of all, for it went after Pharaoh himself by killing his firstborn son. It was also a foreshadowing of the death of God's firstborn son centuries later.[15]

God, Himself, was showing He reigns supreme over any false god who would try to usurp Him.

Appearance of the Kingdom

While Genesis alludes to the kingdom concept, Exodus explicitly screams, "The God of Israel is superior to the gods of Egypt." When God liberated the people from the bondage of Egypt and delivered them through the waters of the Red Sea, Moses sang a praise song to God in Exodus 15 for obliterating "Pharaoh's chariots and his army into the sea; the elite of his officers were drowned in the Red Sea. . . . The floods covered them; they sank to the depths like a stone. . . . Lord, your right hand shattered the enemy. . . . You stretched out your right hand, and the earth swallowed them" (Exod. 15:4–6, 12). This song of victory concludes with the establishment of God's Temple in connection to His kingdom reigning forever. Moses pens the first words about the "kingdom of God" in the Bible.

"You will bring them in and plant them on the mountain of your possession; LORD, you have prepared the place for your *dwelling*; LORD, your hands have established the sanctuary. The LORD will reign forever and ever!" (Exod. 15:17–18). Reigning forever pronounces God's kingship over His people. No longer will the people serve the pharaoh of Egypt. God's chosen people are free now to worship and serve Him.

"Will reign" is an imperfect verb in Hebrew, signifying that the future is up in the air; it's dependent upon some present action. An example of this in English would be, "An apple a day keeps the doctor away." The future isn't actual yet; it is dependent on a present action. The doctor being kept away is dependent on whether you eat an apple a day. Moses is saying that they have observed God's miraculous act of salvation. They have observed first-hand God's glory as King, and His worth is not found in palaces, chariots, gold, or silver. His inheritance is the nation He saved. Because of what they observed, they can say with certainty, "God is reigning today and will reign forever."

Their response for God's gracious act of salvation would be obedience to His Word, which is why the next stop before the Promised Land was a mountain. Was their freedom from the bondage of Egypt the result of their own good works? Did God rescue the nation because they earned it? Did their redemption come about because they would pay God back one day? No. God set them free as a demonstration of His unearned and unmerited favor.

The law was not the prerequisite for redemption; it was given as a gift *after* they were emancipated from Pharaoh's rule. God established His kingdom by proving His majesty and by delivering His people from slavery. And His subjects demonstrate their loyalty by obeying His decrees. It is a joyful adherence to the commands of God in response to what He has already done for them.

Scripture records the whole history of God's people from their beginning in Exodus 15 to their future renewal in Revelation 15. In between is language of the kingdom, a kingdom not coming, but one that is already, to some extent, here.

Notice how believers in Revelation sing the same song of Moses: "They sang the song of God's servant Moses and the song of the Lamb: Great and awe-inspiring are your works, Lord God, the Almighty; just and true are your ways, King of the nations. Lord, who will not fear and glorify your name? For you alone are holy. All the nations will come and worship before you because your righteous acts have been revealed" (Rev. 15:3–4). In one sense, the culmination mirrors the commencement. The good news for all followers of Jesus is that there is no need to wait to enter the kingdom. Jesus instructed His followers two thousand years ago, "Seek first [today] the kingdom" (Matt. 6:33). The end times consummation has broken into the present time. The entire Old Testament message can be summed up in the phrase: "Our God reigns forever and ever."

A Wedding Ceremony

Though the people were overjoyed at God's miraculous display in Egypt, they would soon learn that redemption was not the only goal of their freedom; responsibility was. Passover, the night of their freedom from bondage, was incomplete without Pentecost, the next event in their redemption story. What came after was a covenant they could understand, for it resembled a traditional Israelite marriage ceremony.

Look at the following unfolding of events: three days of sanctification, approaching the mountain, Moses as the mediator, a wedding agreement (the Ten Commandments), and the response of the people (*ketubah*, a marriage agreement, in Hebrew) in Exodus 24:3, "We will do," recreates an image of a wedding ceremony.[16] God redeemed His people in order to reveal His law on Mount Sinai, demanding responsibility on their part to obey it. *Their salvation was unconditional, but the intimacy of their relationship was contingent on their obedience to the agreement.* Both grace and obedience are necessary for a healthy relationship.

The wedding concept is woven throughout the pages of the Bible. God is always portrayed as the bridegroom or husband and His people are the bride.

> Isaiah 54:5: Indeed, your *husband* is your Maker—His name is the LORD of Armies—and the Holy One of Israel is your Redeemer; He is called the God of all the whole Earth.

> Isaiah 62:5: For as a young man *marries* a young woman, so your sons will marry you; and as a groom rejoices over *his bride*, so your God will rejoice over you.

> Jeremiah 3:14: "Return, faithless people," declares the LORD, "for I am your *husband*. I will choose you—one from a town and two from a clan—and bring you to Zion." (NIV)

> Jeremiah 31:31–32: "The days are coming,"
> declares the LORD, "when I will make a new
> covenant with the people of Israel and with the
> people of Judah. It will not be like the covenant
> I made with their ancestors when I took them
> by the hand to lead them out of Egypt, because
> they broke my covenant, though I was a *hus-*
> *band* to them," declares the LORD. (NIV)

The entire book of Hosea explains how Israel prostituted herself out to other gods, and how God, as a loving partner, constantly pursues His bride.

Wedding preparations precede a ceremony, and Israel's engagement was no exception. "Then Moses came down from the mountain to the people and consecrated them, and they washed their clothes. He said to the people, 'Be prepared by the third day. Do not have sexual relations with women'" (Exod. 19:14–15). The Israelites were about to enter into a covenant with God that required them to cleanse themselves for the ceremony before accepting to the vows of the covenant. *God initiated the relationship at Passover, but consummated the relationship on Sinai.* The nation was only able to receive, and subsequently obey, God's commands after He saved them, not before. *God acts; people react.*

Over the course of many days, God would outline 613 commandments for Moses, but ten of them He would write with His own finger on stone tablets. Exodus 20 outlines "The Ten," as some refer to them: 1. You shall have no other gods before Me, 2. You shall not make idols, 3. You shall not take the name of the Lord your God in vain, 4. Remember the Sabbath day, to keep it holy, 5. Honor your father and your mother, 6. You shall not murder, 7. You shall not commit adultery, 8. You shall not steal.

9. You shall not bear false witness against your neighbor, 10. You shall not covet.

These are the vows to the relationship. They were not new commands, nor would they have been a surprise for this expectant bride. Old Testament scholar Walter Kaiser finds all ten of the Commandments in Genesis:

1. The first, Genesis 35:2: "Get rid of the foreign gods."

2. The second, Genesis 31:30: Laban to Jacob: "But why did you steal my gods?"

3. The third, Genesis 24:3: "I want you to swear by the LORD."

4. The fourth, Genesis 2:3: "God blessed the seventh day and made it holy."

5. The fifth, Genesis 27:41: "The days of mourning my father are near."

6. The sixth, Genesis 4:9: "Where is your brother Abel?"

7. The seventh, Genesis 39:9: "How then could I do such a wicked thing and sin against God?"

8. The eighth, Genesis 44:4–7: "Why have you stolen my silver cup?"

9. The ninth, Genesis 39:17: "[Joseph] came to me to make sport of me . . . but . . . he ran. . . ."

10. Genesis 12:18; 20:3: "You are as good as dead because of the woman you have taken; she is a married woman."[17]

The first four commandments speak to our relationship with God, and the final six deal with our relationship with others. The commandments were not unfair restrictions or infringements on their personal liberties; they were revolutionary, counter-cultural decrees. In Egypt the people were tempted by rampant paganism, sexual immorality, selfishness, greed, and lust for power. God was setting a new standard. The law should not be viewed as mere conduct to live by; it was a means for intimacy with a personal God who desired to dwell among His people. Their ultimate obedience to the commands of God was out of devotion, never duty. The commandments were a compass to righteous living and a right relationship with God.

Modern believers may be unaware of the parameters of a biblical covenant. It was a formal contract between two parties who agreed to the terms and conditions set forward. In many ways, it is similar, in a simplified way, to the contracts we sign for cable TV or cellphone service. We agree to the "terms and conditions" in the fine print to hold our end of the bargain.

We may have a casual approach to making contracts today (some of us don't ever read the words), but in the ancient world the contractual obligations pertaining to covenants were not taken lightly. Marriage is an example of a covenant relationship between a man, a woman, and God. We profess love for our spouse while covenanting with God. In this passage, at the birth of God's people as a nation and as a representation of God's kingdom on Earth, Moses functions as mediator between God and the people, a matchmaker if you will.

With tablets in hand, Moses approached the people who were dressed in "white garments," a sign of cleansing and consecration for marriage. He read the *ketubah* contract, the Ten Commandments, to the nation as an invitation to a covenant relationship. The people respond "with a single voice, 'We will do everything that the LORD has commanded'" (Exod. 24:3). Similar to the vow exchange between a husband and a wife, the people shout: "We do!" God not only became their partner, but their king.

Consequently, the Torah (the Word of God) reveals the character of the King and the guidelines for a right relationship with Him. Dwight Pryor explains, "Within this frame of reference, the Torah is understood to be: 1. A gracious gift—given to a redeemed people and received in love, 2. A treasure—that delights, satisfies and restores the soul, 3. Written by the 'finger of God'—i.e., by the fire and the power of the Spirit, and 4. Guidance and instruction—given by a loving Father to His children, that they may live long and prosper in the place divinely appointed for them."[18]

While Abraham accepted the yoke of the kingdom when God called him, the nation of Israel accepted the yoke of the kingdom at Sinai.[19] It is a relationship that will permeate the entirety of Scripture from this point forward.

Redemption, Revelation, Responsibility

Even though God is king over the world He created, his kingship is distinct among a people whom He redeemed. Agreement to the marriage covenant on Mt. Sinai was more than lip service. The people were expected to respond with loyalty by keeping God's commandments through daily living, and by doing this, God's kingdom agenda would advance throughout the world. The formula is as follows: *God redeemed on Passover to reveal Himself to them on Mt. Sinai in order to have a relationship with them through their responsibility to obey His commands.*

This same paradigm is followed in the Gospel accounts with the calling of the twelve apostles. Jesus proved throughout His ministry that He was the Moses-like figure who would accomplish what Moses fell short of doing by leading the people not into the Promised Land, but into the kingdom of God. Many similarities can be made between the two: both were shepherds (Moses in his profession; Jesus in his ministry, see John 10:11), both led the people out of bondage; both were hidden in Egypt as children; both fasted for forty days; both selected twelve men; and both fed the people with bread in the wilderness.

It's no wonder that when Jesus outlines what living looks like in His kingdom, He mimics Moses by ascending a mountain (Matt. 5:1). Notice what Jesus did immediately before sharing the Sermon on the Mount. He selected the twelve disciples, according to Mark 3 and Luke 6. They didn't choose Him; He choose them. As already seen, redemption precedes responsibility. Another way to say it is that grace from God precedes work for God. Jesus concludes the Sermon by stating the importance of obeying the words He just shared.[20] Obedience to the commands of Christ is not legalism. "Legalism says, 'I must obey God in order to be saved.' Grace says, 'I must obey because I am saved.'"[21]

The same is true today. God saved us apart from any good deed we could offer. "All have sinned and fallen short of the glory of God," Paul explained in Romans 3:23. He added in the book of Ephesians, "You were dead in your trespasses and sins. . . . For you are saved by grace through faith, and this is not from yourselves; it is God's gift—not from works, so that no one can boast" (Eph. 2:1, 8–9). Although God redeemed us by His gracious initiative, He expects us to live for Him through obedience. Paul doesn't end his thought with verse nine. He continues, "For we are his workmanship, created in Christ Jesus for good works, which God prepared ahead of time for us to do" (Eph. 2:10). We are not saved by good works, but we will do good works after being saved because of the relationship we have been brought into.

Paul's language about the crossroads between life and death is not new. God presented the same offer for his people just entering this covenant relationship: "See, today I have set before you life and prosperity, death and adversity" (Deut. 30:15). How would the people live in prosperity under the kingship of God? He explains in the next verse, "For I am commanding you today to love the LORD your God, *to walk in his ways, and to keep his commands, statutes, and ordinances,* so that you may live and multiply, and the LORD your God may bless you in the land you are entering to possess" (Deut. 30:16).

Walking with God has always been His *modus operandi.* He walked with Adam, Enoch, and Abraham. He enlisted Moses to lead the people on a forty-year walk, where He would journey alongside them. Joshua carried the baton into the Promised Land by treading through town after town declaring God's rule and reign. Jesus used the walking motif in the New Testament when He summoned His future disciples to follow Him or "walk after me" (Matt. 4:19). When Thomas questioned Him about following Him to the place He is preparing in heaven, Jesus didn't point him to a path, like every other religious figure in history, by saying, "This is the way." He exclaimed, "*I am* the way."

Early Christians in the book of Acts were referred to as "the Way," as revealed in Acts: "But Saul, still breathing threats and murder against the disciples of the Lord, went to the high priest and asked him for letters to the synagogues at Damascus, so that if he found any belonging to *the Way,* men or women, he might bring them bound to Jerusalem" (9:1–2 RSV), and Acts 19, "But when some became stubborn and continued in unbelief, speaking evil of *the Way* before the congregation, he withdrew from them and took the disciples with Him, reasoning daily in the hall of Tyrannus" (19:9 ESV). *The Way* describes someone who acknowledges God as king and submits to His rule over his or her life by walking after Him.

Faith in Action

Faith, for the Hebrew, is not memorizing a set of facts to pass a theological assessment administered by a pastor before baptism. Faith always manifests itself with action, which is why James emphasized the point in his epistle: "But someone will say, 'You have faith, and I have works.' Show me your faith without works, and I will show you faith by my works. You believe that God is one. Good! Even the demons believe—and they shudder" (James 2:18). Demons believe in God but don't worship and serve Him. True faith must be more than mere intellectual understanding.

The first occurrence of the word *faith* in the Old Testament is found in Exodus 17:11–13: "While Moses held up his hand, Israel prevailed, but whenever he put his hand down, Amalek prevailed. When Moses' hands grew heavy, they took a stone and put it under him, and he sat down on it. Then Aaron and Hur supported his hands, one on one side and one on the other so that his hands remained steady [*emunah*] until the sun went down. So Joshua defeated Amalek and his army with the sword." "Emunah" can be translated as steadfastness or faithfulness, as seen in Jeremiah 5:3, "LORD, don't your eyes look for faithfulness?" and Habakkuk 2:4, "The righteous one will live by his faith [faithfulness]."

Further evidence is seen in Hebrews 11 where belief is accompanied with action. This chapter is called the "Hall of Faith," which signifies "faithfulness." Each man is remembered for what he did, not what he knew intellectually. Faith, in a Hellenistic, Western culture, is normally thought of as agreeing to creeds and catechisms. I do not mean to imply that orthodoxy is not important. It is. But let's not favor orthodoxy, what we believe, to the extent that we neglect orthopraxy, how we act. When the religious leaders inquired about who their neighbor was, Jesus didn't distribute a how-to manual for categorizing good and bad neighbors. He shared a story about what a neighbor "does." He stops for an injured man, tends to his wounds, and He cares for his needs.

The reason God brought Israel out of Egypt was so that they would worship Him and Him alone. In establishing this relationship with them, He not only wanted them to worship Him; He wanted to dwell with them. As already mentioned, we see this from the fact that thirteen entire chapters are spent on how to construct the tabernacle (compared to the two on how he created the world).

God is a God who desires to break into civilization. He came down to be with Adam. He came down on Sinai. He came down in His Son Jesus. And He will come down at the end of days. We're trying to leave the world; God entering in. It's why Exodus begins with a departure and ends with a tabernacle.

CHAPTER 3

The Epicenter of Judaism: The Temple

I grew up watching wrestling. I'd watch in awe as Hulk Hogan leaned heavily into the ropes and launched himself at his opponent, who would be sent sprawling in a dramatic flail. I'd watch Jeff Jarrett, known as Double J, grab his guitar and smash it over someone's noggin, or The Rock pick up the microphone after a spectacular victory and ask if the crowd could smell what The Rock was cooking? The outrageous storylines, the drama between wrestlers, the surprise entrances, and the shocking twists captivated me.

Sure, it wasn't "quality" television, but professional wrestling is all about the spectacle. Fortunately for me, my two sons have caught the fever I had at their age. They love tussling on the carpet while watching the exciting footage on the screen. But their love was based only on what they'd seen on the TV in our living room. It was nothing compared to seeing a live match.

I eventually got to take Rig and Ryder to their first WrestleMania, the Super Bowl of wrestling. In that moment, they were more excited than I'd ever seen them in their lives.

They were surrounded by thousands of uproarious fans cheering on guys, and girls, doing backflips off of ropes, delivering spectacular submission holds, and performing signature moves to the loud approval of everyone looking on. Watching a wrestling match on television cannot compare with watching it live in person.

I want to take you back in time to a place you may have heard about—possibly through Sunday school handouts or pictures in books, maybe by reading descriptions in the Old Testament, or by seeing parts portrayed in popular media—but have never truly experienced. As we visit the tabernacle and discover what it represents, the kingdom of God at hand comes into focus.

A Brief History of the Temple

"The Tabernacle," according to A. B. Simpson, "is the greatest of all the Old Testament types of Christ. It was all one great object lesson of spiritual truth."[22] Before the permanent Temple was built, God instructed Moses to construct a traveling structure for meeting with him. Many believers view this as a tent that contains various pieces of furniture, or a tedious section of Scripture to wade through in the Old Testament. The most remarkable fact about the tabernacle is that it reveals God's desire to come down and be in the midst of His people. When John, and Jesus after him, proclaimed that the kingdom of God was at hand, they were not talking about a place we go after death—they were referring to a place, a person, and a power that is available to us in this present moment.

If you or I were privileged to live during the Second Temple period—the period from 538 BC to the destruction of the

Temple by the Roman Empire during the Jewish-Roman War in AD 70, according to many scholars—you would have seen a true marvel of the world. I want to take you on a journey through history to look at the Temple.

The Temple During Jesus' Day

God has always desired to dwell among His people. After redeeming them from the bondage of the Egyptians, God instructed Moses, "Let them make me a sanctuary, that I may dwell in their midst" (Exod. 25:8 ESV). So the Israelites built a tabernacle that could travel with them during their nomadic days in the desert. After generations, under the kingship of Solomon, a permanent Temple replaced the tabernacle. What happened to the tabernacle? Roger Liebi, in his book *The Messiah and the Temple*, comments,

> The Tabernacle with all its furniture was brought to Jerusalem (1 Kings 8:4; 1 Chr. 5:5). . . . The Tabernacle, as a construction which could be

taken apart, was placed in the depths of the
Temple Mount, right under the cavities of the
Holy Place (BT sotah 9a). The Temple furniture
of the Tabernacle was used further in the First
Temple.[23]

Solomon completed the construction of this Temple after
seven years and seven months of labor in 967 BC. At first he
divided thirty thousand Israelites into three groups before enlist-
ing 153,600 workers—according to 1 Kings 7:15–17—to carry,
cut, and supervise the stone work. Providentially, the site for the
construction was the same spot where God directed Abraham to
offer up his son Isaac (see Gen. 22:2 and 2 Chron. 3:1).

The structure stood for almost four hundred years after its
completion until 586 BC when the Babylonians sieged the city
under the leadership of King Nebuchadnezzar. During the time
leading up to when Israel would be captives in Babylon, the
prophets Isaiah, Jeremiah, and Ezekiel prophesied to the people
that the Temple would be rebuilt and the Israelites would be
gathered again. After the Babylonians loot the Temple treasures,
the Ark of the Covenant is never returned to the Holy of Holies
again. From the time of Ezra in the fifth-century BC to the
destruction of the Temple in AD 70, nothing occupies the room
behind the second curtain Temple, a fact many Christians may
not know.[24] Those in the inner sanctum who knew about this
must have realized something was terribly wrong, but the thirst
for power and control has a way of silencing problems, as we will
see with the rise of the corrupt Sadducean sect.

Ezra, Nehemiah, and Zerrubabel partnered together to
lead the charge to return to Jerusalem to rebuild the Temple.
Nehemiah heard about the destruction of the city while he was
serving in the court of the king, wept over it, and appealed to the

pagan King Artaxerxes for a leave of absence so that he might
assist in the rebuilding process. The king graciously approved
his request, and Nehemiah saw the walls restored. As soon as the
people settled back into the routines of the Temple, Antiochus,
in the fourth century, looted and defiled it. In 167 BC, robbers
ransacked the Temple of all the gold, blasphemed God by erect-
ing a statue of the Greek god Jupiter inside, and desecrated it
by sacrificing pigs, a non-kosher animal, on the altar. They also
forced Jews to eat swine. The once-thriving nation had delved
into the depths of despair and despondency.

As grim as it appeared, though, God had set the stage for
a family to intervene and restore the Temple to a working condition before God sent His Messiah. What Daniel predicted
hundreds of years before had come to fruition: "His [Antiochus
Epiphanies] forces will rise up and desecrate the temple fortress.
They will abolish the regular sacrifice and set up the abomination of desolation. With flattery he will corrupt those who act
wickedly toward the covenant, but the people who know their
God will be strong and take action" (Dan. 11:31–32). Within
the Temple, it was imperative for Jews to rightly worship God
according to Deuteronomy 12.

Metafius Maccabeus, having endured enough defilement,
took matters into his own hands. After being forced to eat pig
one day, he, along with his five sons, revolted against the Greek
soldiers. When he stabbed a guard, a revolution began to reclaim
the Temple for the Jewish people. In 164 BC, the Maccabeans,
led by Metafius's son Judas, won a battle that can only be
explained as miraculous. The eight-day celebration of Hanukkah
still commemorates the battle that was won by the Maccabean
family and the rededication of the Temple.

In 37 BC Herod the Great became king of Israel. He was plagued by the fear of losing his throne, and his actions proved it. He murdered his wife, strangled his sons, and poisoned family and friends to preserve his empire. Caesar Augustus commented on his monarchy: "It's safer to be a pig in Herod's house than one of his sons."[25] It was Herod's desire to be remembered. This desire motivated him to extend the platform of the Temple, making it one of the wonders of the world. The renovation project began in 20 BC, just sixteen years before the birth of Christ. The gigantic structure overwhelmed worshippers as they ascended the Temple Mount and thrusted Jerusalem into the spotlight of the day. All the attention year after year, feast after feast, and day after day converged at one site: Mount Moriah, where Abraham offered up Isaac, where the Temple was built, and where Jesus would give himself up as the spotless sinless lamb for our sins. The stage is now set for the sending of God's Son.

To grasp how important the Temple was to Jesus and His apostles, notice how John described the manner in which Jesus came to the Earth in the opening chapter of John's Gospel: "And the Word became flesh and dwelt among us, and we have seen his glory, glory as of the only Son from the Father, full of grace and truth" (John 1:14 ESV). When selecting a term to describe the incarnation, John chose *dwelt*, which can be translated as "tabernacled." If you remember, the tabernacle was the first iteration of the Temple, where God on High would come down and reside in the midst of His people. The reason David could say, "Better a day in your courts than a thousand anywhere else," is because God dwelt in the Temple. From the onset of His life, Jesus was deeply connected to the Temple.

The Temple and Jesus

The word *temple* is used one hundred times in the New Testament, sixty of which are in the Gospels alone. It was the epicenter of Jewish spirituality. Jesus would have first laid eyes on the Temple as a baby when His parents dedicated Him to the Lord in Luke 2:22–24. He would have grown up anticipating the journeys His family made into the heart of Jerusalem for feast days. He would have been overwhelmed by the contrast between Nazareth, where He lived, and Jerusalem. Nazareth was a small, insignificant village with a population of around two or three hundred people. The town was so insignificant that early maps didn't even include it. Farm land and hills surrounded the city. Jesus, as a small-town boy, would have stood in awe as He absorbed the magnitude of His father's house.

When Satan selected a location for tempting Jesus, he brought Him to the pinnacle of the Temple (Matt. 4:5) because it was the most magnificent location Jesus could have stood. Jesus cleansed the Temple of the corrupt practices of the money-changers (Matt. 21:12; John 2:16). Jesus spent time in the Temple among the Sages as a young boy (Luke 2:41–52). He taught in the Temple (Luke 21). As He overlooked the Temple from the Mount of Olives, He wept over the city (Luke 19:41). The Temple was crucial to Jesus' life and ministry.

A reverence for the Temple didn't cease with the death of Jesus. He "led them out to the vicinity of Bethany, and lifting up his hands he blessed them. And while he was blessing them, he left them and was carried up into heaven. After worshiping him, they returned to Jerusalem with great joy. And they were continually in the *temple* praising God" (Luke 24:50–53). The early church met "every day," and they "devoted themselves to meeting together in the *temple*, and broke bread from house to house. They ate their food with joyful and sincere hearts, praising God and enjoying the favor of all the people. Every day the Lord added to their number those who were being saved" (Acts 2:46–47). You may think the apostles went to the Temple to hand out tracts (a twentieth-century invention) or lead people in the sinner's prayer (a nineteenth-century invention) after Jesus' death, but that is incorrect. Each was raised going to the Temple to worship, so they continued going as was their custom.

The Temple was important to the Jewish people, the Temple was important to Jesus, and the Temple was important to the apostles. What I want you to see is how an understanding of the Temple should impact us today.

The Temple and You

Because of God's promise to David in 1 Chronicles, first-century believers expected the Messiah to build God's Temple when He arrived: "I will raise up after you your descendent, who is one of your own sons, and I will establish his kingdom. He is the one who will build a house for me, and I will establish his throne forever. I will be his father, and he will be my son" (1 Chron. 17:11–13). Although the passage speaks directly of Solomon, we now know it to be a foreshadowing of the "son of David" or the Messiah. When Jesus said He would destroy the Temple and rebuild it, the crowd heard a messianic claim from Jesus. Where they missed the point, though, was in thinking the Temple was a building made of mortar and brick; in reality, the Temple is constructed of men and women who are filled with God's Spirit. The same way God filled the tabernacle and Solomon's Temple with His presence, He fills born-again believers at the moment of salvation.

When describing the new relationship that Christ secured through His death on the cross, Paul invokes Temple imagery when speaking to the believers in Corinth: "Don't you yourselves know that you are God's temple and that the Spirit of God lives in you? If anyone destroys God's temple, God will destroy him; for God's temple is holy, and that is what you are" (1 Cor. 3:16–17). Westerners unfamiliar with the landscape of the Temple lose the weight of these words. In 1 Corinthians, Paul was writing to Gentiles, and in this passage he did something absolutely remarkable: he included them in something that they would have seen and heard about, but could not partake in. Labeling someone God's Temple is an honor unlike any other. Those who were once far from God are now conduits of His presence. Believers's bodies are likened to the most Holy place on the planet to the Jewish nation. God's presence now resides within them as a result of Jesus' death, burial, and resurrection.

Paul says later in this letter, "Don't you know that your body is a temple of the Holy Spirit who is in you, whom you have from God?" (1 Cor. 6:19). Unfortunately, without an understanding of the language Paul was using, some have trivialized Paul's words by making them admonitions against drinking, tattoos, or smoking for fear of blaspheming the Temple (our body) of God. However, the word for "your" in this passage is plural, not singular. Paul is addressing the church as a whole, not individuals. In chapter 11, he describes how each member is a part of the larger church body. Believers comprise the collective body of the Temple of God.

Am I discounting the importance of caring for one's physical body through exercise, healthy eating, and holiness? By no means. Every believer should examine his or her life physically, emotionally, and spiritually in light of how it affects the larger body of Christ. What Paul meant, though, is the Temple became mobile as the people of God became the church. They were not constrained to a particular location any longer.

A monumental event that took place during Jesus' ministry was His cleansing of the Temple, when He purged His Father's house of the unholy business practices of the so-called religious leaders. Jesus cleansed the Temple of moneychangers who took over the Gentile court that allowed other nations to observe the worship of the one, true God.

In a sense, we must regularly do the same thing. Perpetual examination of our spiritual life is important to examine what crowds out worship of God. Christ takes up residence in our lives after salvation through the indwelling of the Holy Spirit, and we must be honorable vessels in order to be useful to the master (2 Tim. 2:21). He desires to occupy every aspect of our lives.

C. S. Lewis explains what Christ communicates to us: "Give me all. I don't want so much of your time and so much of your money and so much of your work: I want you. I have not come to torment your natural self, but to kill. No half measures are any good. I don't want to cut off a branch here and branch there, I want to have the whole tree down. Hand over the whole natural self. . . . I will give you a new self instead. In fact, I will give you myself: My own will shall become yours."[26] May these words resonate in our minds constantly.

CHAPTER 4

Hellenism, Israel, and the Priesthood

After the Temple was established as the centerpiece of Judaism, the Greeks hijacked both the building and the Levitical system that supported it. We've seen a picture of the history of that Temple—it is nothing short of miraculous, so the system that corrupted it must have been massive and powerful. For us to grasp the impact of Jesus' ministry on Earth and have a greater, personal understanding of Him, we must place ourselves back into the context of the world He entered. What was the ancient world like?

Influence of Hellenism

The climate of the first century was volatile and tumultuous. The Roman Empire had conquered the world with one military dictatorship controlling the lands that border the Mediterranean Sea. They taxed their people heavily and encouraged an atmosphere of polytheism, idol worship, and loose living. It was not just brute force that oppressed everyone under their control; it was also their value system.

Prior to the rise of the Roman Empire, Alexander the Great, a bright and promising twenty-year-old, assumed power after his father Philip II was assassinated in 336 BC. In fewer than ten years, he would conquer the known world with a strategy unlike any before or after. After besieging the cities of Tyre and Sidon, Alexander marched toward Jerusalem on his way to Egypt. The High Priest of Israel met him at the border expecting a massacre but was surprised by Alexander's request to offer sacrifices to Yahweh. The Priest guided him through the process of offering an acceptable sacrifice to God in order to curb any criticism from the people.[27]

This was a remarkable irony. It caught the Jewish leadership off guard. One would have expected such a dominant leader to walk in, forcefully change things around to the way that he wants them, and then leave people in charge of keeping it that way. But what the Jewish leaders didn't know was that prior to entering Jerusalem, Alexander was briefed on the prophecies in the book of Daniel, which displayed a Greek destroying the Persian Empire. John Anderson explains some of these intricate details: "It is important to note the fine detail of the historical fulfillment of the dream recorded in Daniel 8. The goat (the Greco-Macedonian kingdom) that destroyed the ram (the Medo-Persian Empire) had 'a notable horn' that represented its first king, Alexander the Great (Dan. 8:21). The dream also related that when this horn was broken, four smaller horns representing four other kingdoms were to arise in its place (v. 22)."[28]

Alexander understood the Jewish wariness of a powerful Greek man, so he adopted an air of openness to their worldview. He did this so fluently that people viewed him as a friend of the

Jewish people.[29] Before you relax your guard against this pagan ruler, let me remind you of his method. His actions provide insight into his strategy for world domination. Where most rulers would come in and take a people by force (as the Romans and Persians before did), Alexander offered his captives a plethora of choices. Built into the Greek worldview was a flat-out acceptance of anything someone wanted to believe, as can be glimpsed by the Pantheon's twelve Olympian gods: Jupiter, Juno, Neptune, Ceres, Minerva, Apollo, Diana (Artemis in Greek), Mars, Venus, Vulcan, Mercury, Vesta, and Bacchus (Dionysus in Greek).

How Alexander Infiltrated the World

Alexander did not conquer by brute force. His infiltration was sly. He implemented a mind-set influenced by the institutions and philosophers of his day which transformed the world's culture by focusing on four areas: *education, athletics, information*, and *entertainment*. His first step was to set up schools wherever he went to teach world religions, Greek mythology, world history, astronomy, mathematics, philosophy, and just about anything else that could be taught. He advocated for the broadening of educational horizons—something that appeared exciting and new to Jews who had received every one of their educational lessons for their entire life from their Scriptures.

But importantly, under Alexander's system they were not prohibited from learning the Scriptures; in fact, Jews were encouraged to continue studying them. The important distinction was that things pertaining to Yahweh were now just one more option in a system of equally weighted choices. He erected libraries next to synagogues and heralded words such as, "Keep learning what you've been learning, but don't stop there! Don't be closed-minded; let us help you expand your minds!" His tactics were so subtle that most Jews didn't realize they had been infected until it was too late.

His second step was to introduce athletics. The Greeks invented competitive sports as we know them today, and they caught on so quickly and efficiently that the Isthmian Games—the predecessors to our present-day Olympic Games—were the basis of one of Paul's chief metaphors for the Christian life: "Don't you know that the runners in a stadium all race, but only one receives the prize? Run in such a way to win the prize" (1 Cor. 9:24). Paul wrote this not because he was Hellenistic but because the people at the church in Corinth, where the games were held, were fluent in the language of sports. Corinth, after all, was where athletes participated in the renowned Isthmian Games. The obsession with athletics introduced something into Jewish culture that was previously a foreign concept: competition. You will be hard pressed to find a *Jewish Book of World Records.* "Why would I want to compete against my brother? He labors alongside me for the same cause against the same enemy." After the introduction of athletics, Jews were drawn to the Decapolis to watch men compete against each other in the games.

His third step was to introduce outposts for the dissemination of information. He brought access to world events, politics, art, music, and news to a culture that was previously—intentionally—set apart from the world. Prior to Alexander's influence, Jews cared little about the world at large. Soon, though, they had rugs, furs, and commodities imported from all over the world adorning their homes. Pottery and furnishings were sold and traded in Greek-controlled stations throughout the land. While there is nothing wrong with this in itself, these subtle changes led to many Israelites diverting their focus from the things of God and placing it on any of the myriad of distractions around them. God's people were always meant to be a light to the nations, but during this period, some—though not all—became fascinated by the nations and enticed to their way of doing things.

Alexander's final step was to introduce theater into everyday life. The Greeks invented tragedy and comedy plays as we know them today that serve as the basis of the design for our modern theaters. Even the word *hypocrite*, as used by Jesus in Matthew 6, is a Greek term borrowed to describe the masks that certain actors and actresses wore during a play. We need only look around us today to understand the ramifications that easily accessible entertainment takes on the spiritual life of someone seeking to follow God.

While I'm not advocating against entertainment for the purposes of relaxation and enjoyment, I do want you to be cognizant of the indoctrination, albeit subtle at times, that movies, television shows, and the Internet have on humans. The Jews enjoyed entertainment through participating in the festivals. However, their celebration was with God and the community of faith rather than apart from Him. In contrast, theater, as well as modern forms of entertainment, was enjoyed passively and individually.

Time that Jews may have otherwise spent memorizing Scripture or repeating a lesson could now be spent watching performances at the theater. It's worth pointing out the similarity between Alexander's influence and the influence that Hollywood, secular educational institutions, media outlets, and athletics have on our society. This, of course, isn't to say that we should live in holy huddles. There is a time and a place and a way in which to enjoy some of the creativity, art, and entertainment that the world displays. But we are always to do this as Christians, never as passive consumers of whatever the world throws at us.

A Volatile Landscape

By the second-century BC, Hellenism dominated the entire Western known world. Greek culture infiltrated the Jewish culture so much that in 260 BC, Greek-speaking Jews went to work translating the Hebrew Scriptures into the language of the world under the direction of King Ptolemy. Most secular scholars agree that the work was complete by 250 BC, etching more than three hundred prophetic utterances about the birth, life, death, and resurrection of the Christ in the annuals of history 250 years before his arrival.

Much of the Greek history and influence of Hellenism is recorded in the Apocryphal books of the Maccabees. The first chapter (1 Macc. 1:10–15) describes the subtle influence of the wicked ruler Antiochus Epiphanes, king of Syria in 167 BC:

> At that time there appeared in the land of Israel a group of traitorous Jews who had no regard for the Law and who had a bad influence on many of our people. They said, "Let's come to terms with the Gentiles, for our refusal to associate with them has brought us nothing but trouble." This proposal appealed to many people, and some of them became so enthusiastic about it that they went to the king and received from him permission to follow Gentile customs. They built in Jerusalem a stadium like those in the Greek cities. They had surgery performed to hide their circumcision, abandoned the holy covenant, started associating with Gentiles, and did all sorts of other evil things.

Ephiphanes, which translates "god manifest," (he was clearly a humble man), continued his influence upon the people by issuing "a decree that all nations in his empire should abandon their own customs and become one people. All the Gentiles and even many of the Israelites submitted to this decree. They adopted the official pagan religion, offered sacrifices to idols, and no longer observed the Sabbath" (1 Macc. 1:41–43). The Second Temple was desecrated on December 6, 167 BC, when Antiochus IV ordered the sacrifice of pigs upon the altar of God to pagan gods. Additionally, he erected a statue of Zeus in the Temple. It's easy to see why so many people rose up to claim the title Messiah during this time.

N. T. Wright describes the volatile landscape during this period:

> We know of ten or a dozen other movements that arose in Palestine within about a hundred years either side of Jesus. There seem to have been lots of other young Jews who were prepared to risk all at the head of a little revolutionary group, in the hope that their God would act through them and bring in his kingdom. One of the best known was a man called Judas the Galilean, who led an uprising around the time of Jesus' birth. He and hundreds of others were picked up by the authorities, and they were crucified (Josephus, *Antiquities*, 17:271–98; *War*, 2:56–79). Almost exactly a hundred years after Jesus' death, there was another great revolution, led by Simeon ben-Kosiba. Some of the leading Jewish teachers said "Here at last is the Messiah!" He, too, like all the rest, was hunted

down by the authorities, and killed. In each
case, the death of the leader meant the end of
the movement. The exception proves the rule:
Judas the Galilean seems to have had a family,
to whom his disappointed followers turned.
One of the would-be messiahs during the Jewish
War of 66–70 was a man called Menahem, the
leader of the Sicarii, the dagger-men. He was
the grandson of Judas the Galilean. When he
was killed by a rival group of Jews, a relative
called Eleazar took up the leadership. The group
ended its days on Masada, finally committing
mass suicide when the Romans closed in.[30]

The Maccabeans, or Hasmoneans as they were called, ran
into a problem after assuming control of the Temple. They didn't
have a right to take the throne of God because they were not
descendants of David the king or Aaron the priest. The dynasty
would eventually fall when a civil war erupted between the two
brothers battling for the throne in Jerusalem. Before Jesus arrives
on the scene, the Temple falls into the hands of corrupt, power-
driven men.

A Corrupt Priesthood

Corruption trickled into the priesthood with the appoint-
ment of Jason, the first illegal priest, by Antiochus. Antiochus
accepted money for the position in order to repay the Romans
their enormous tribute—thus ousting Onias III, Jason's brother.
Jason was unqualified to hold the office since he was not a
Zadokian (righteous descendants from the lineage of Eleazer son
of Aaron) descendant. His position was short-lived. In 171 BC,

another non-Zadokian priest bought the office for more money than was previously offered. "This change," according to Lieibi, "marked the downfall of the Zadokian office of high priest. No one can conclusively demonstrate that, after this event, a member of the Zadokian line ever became priest again."[31] The stage is set for what will follow.

The time line speaks for itself. (See Appendix 2 for a list of the Priests of the Old Testament.) Israel was led by forty-three High Priests from the time of Aaron to Onias, the final qualified Zadokian priest, over the course of 1388 years (1560 BC to 172 BC). Thirty-eight high priests occupied the position over the next 242 years. It went from an inherited position to a purchased position. Rampant greed and corruption trickled down to the first century with no high priest rightfully occupying the position during Jesus' day. Thus, we can say that Caiaphas, the high priest of Israel, occupied a position illegally as he handed down the sentence that led to Jesus' death.

Using this as motivation to study the Scriptures and prepare the way for the Messiah, a group of priests moved their families to the Qumran. We know them as the Essenes. The Essenes departed from Israel by and large because of the corruption in the priesthood. Imagine for a moment the tension in the land prior to John the Baptist crying out in the wilderness that the king himself is coming. Everyone knew something must change.

Ultimately, the corruption of the priesthood led to the destruction of the Temple. Tempted to worship other things, the people lost their love for God. The Second Temple (Zerubbabel, Ezra, and Nehemiah) was destroyed in AD 70 by the Romans during the first Jewish Roman War, which was the result of internal strife among the Jews.[32] A lack of love for one another led to its demise. Interestingly enough, Jesus summed the entire law, all 613 commandments of the Torah, into two: love God and love others as yourself.

The scene is set for someone to re-right the wrongs of God's people. Everyone longed for the day when God would restore Israel. Tom Jones and Steve Brown, in their book *The Kingdom of God*, describe the two prevailing beliefs toward the kingdom: "(1) Most believed that the coming of the Kingdom would be so dramatic and decisive that everything on earth would change, with Israel being in complete control, or (2) some may have believed that its coming would be so cataclysmic that history itself would come to an end with the Kingdom being all that was left."[33] Anna's testimony summarized the same belief as she laid eyes on baby Jesus in the Temple: "At that very moment, she came up and began to thank God and to speak about him to all who were looking forward to the redemption of Jerusalem" (Luke 2:38). Little does she know that Jesus' kingdom ministry will reach beyond the borders of Jerusalem.

The Kingdom Among Us

CHAPTER 5

The Kingdom Come

In the first century, two major forces affected the nation of Israel negatively: the widespread corruption in the Sadduceean priesthood and the extensive Roman oppression. All of Israel was awaiting the coming kingdom of God and with it the long-awaited peace and justice to the encumbered nation. They were expecting God to reign over Israel once again as He did in former days and return it to a proper theocracy. They eagerly awaited the day when He would bring judgment and punishment for all unrighteous acts committed against the nation and God. All knew what to look for. The sign of His arrival would be marked by the return of an Elijah-like figure. We recognize this figure as John the Baptist—the one preparing the way of the Lord.

The Kingdom Has Arrived

Shortly after John the Baptist was imprisoned for pointing out the obvious sin of Herod Antipas with Herodias, he dispatched a message to Jesus through His disciples inquiring about the delay in sending the cavalry to rescue him. He demanded,

"Are you the one who is to come, or should we expect someone else?" (Matt. 11:3). The "coming one" was a messianic title for the inauguration of God's kingdom that came from two Old Testament passages: Malachi 3:1–2 and Zechariah 9:9. (For an in depth study of this concept see *The Forgotten Jesus*.) In both accounts, the phrase "coming one" is used to describe the coming kingdom of God. John is not doubting Jesus' identity. What he is doing is questioning His messianic agenda. He is expecting fire from heaven against Israel's enemies and judgment for all sinners. "Jesus, if you're the Messiah, why am I still in prison?"

At this point, John the Baptist's ministry was more widely known than Jesus'. His message was one of fire and judgment for those unwilling to turn from their sins. Unapologetically, he asserted, "[You] Brood of vipers! Who warned you to flee from the coming wrath? Therefore produce fruit consistent with repentance. And don't presume to say to yourselves, 'We have Abraham as our father.' For I tell you that God is able to raise up children for Abraham from these stones. The ax is already at the root of the trees. Therefore, every tree that doesn't produce good fruit will be cut down and thrown into the fire" (Matt. 3:7–10). Signs of the time of the kingdom's arrival will be death, mourning, recompense, and pain. Unfortunately, John's perspective was skewed.

Jesus sent John's disciples back with Scriptures quotations from Isaiah 35 and Isaiah 61: "Go and report to John what you hear and see: The blind receive their sight, the lame walk, those with leprosy are cleansed, the deaf hear, the dead are raised, and the poor are told the good news, and blessed is the one who isn't offended by me" (Matt. 11:4–6). At first glance, it appears Jesus is trying to inspire John with positive reports of His earthly ministry. But by telling John these things, He was using prophecy to correct John's kingdom confusion. The good news of the kingdom is not destruction and damnation for the wicked and rebellious; it's mercy and grace for the hopeless and helpless. Jesus emphasized kingdom activity as proof that the revolution had begun. God's kingdom was here and now.

When John's messengers left, Jesus turned to the crowd for a teaching moment: "This is the one about whom it is written: See, I am sending my messenger ahead of you; he will prepare your way before you. Truly I tell you, among those born of women no one greater than John the Baptist has appeared, but the least in the kingdom of heaven is greater than he. From the days of John the Baptist until now, the kingdom of heaven has been suffering violence, and the violent have been seizing it by force. For all the prophets and the law prophesied until John. And if you're willing to accept it, he is the Elijah who is to come. Let anyone who has ears listen" (Matt. 11:10–15). By quoting Malachi 3, Jesus identified John as the prophet who would prepare the way for the coming kingdom. John the Baptist was never able to join the movement of Christ. He was given a mission, and he was faithful to it, but he sadly died in prison before he could become a disciple. He never became one of Jesus' disciples. Yes, he pointed people to Jesus, but he never became a follower of Jesus.

However, John was greater than all the prophets who came before him because he was the final prophet to predict the arrival of the King. Jesus time stamped the beginning of the kingdom and the king's arrival according to John's earthly ministry.

We know this from John's pronouncement of the gospel. "Good news" was heralded by a person when a king would come to town. The messenger would go before the procession and clear the streets so the honored guest could enter. "The Greek word for gospel, *euanggelion*, (literally "good news") in the New Testament," according to Lois Tverberg, "also comes from terminology that was used in regards to kings and their dominions. When a new king was crowned, the *euanggelion* was the announcement that the monarch had taken the throne, that a new kingdom had taken power."[34] John's ministry paved the way for King Jesus' arrival.

The Kingdom Force

Does the kingdom break into the world violently? The New King James Version translates Matthew 11:12: "And from the days of John the Baptist until now the kingdom of heaven *suffers violence*, and *the violent take it by force*." Devoid of chapter references or verse numbers, first-century Rabbis often made connections to the Old Testament by quoting a phrase or verse. The hearer's mind jogged through their mental file cabinets to the exact location of the cross-reference.[35] According to Pryor, Jesus had Micah 2 in mind when He spoke Matthew 11:12.[36] The Sages of Israel viewed this passage as a Messianic prophecy:[37]

> I will indeed gather all of you, Jacob;
> I will collect the remnant of Israel.
> I will bring them together like sheep in a pen,
> like a flock in the middle of its pasture.
> It will be noisy with people.
> One who *breaks open the way* will advance
>   before them;
> they will break out, pass through the city gate,
>   and leave by it.
> Their King will pass through before them,
> the LORD their leader. (Micah 2:12–13)

God Himself will come to gather the people together; however, one will precede Him to "break open" the way for the sheep to go out. At night a shepherd would corral the sheep in a pen or rock cave to protect them from predators. He then either slept by the doorway or pinned up a gate with rocks. In the morning, he kicked over the rocks in order for the sheep to go forth and eat in the field. By quoting this passage, Jesus is saying that after the gate is opened, the King of the kingdom will go before them.

Additionally, by referencing John the Baptist in conjunction with the kingdom breaking forth, Jesus envisioned His movement multiplying forcefully or powerfully, not violently or destructively. Remember, John is the forerunner that Malachi spoke of who prepares the way for the king (see Mal. 3:1–2). He "broke open the *way*" so the sheep can go free. Does one enter the kingdom by might? Does one take hold of the blessings with strength? No. Entrance into the kingdom is through repentance, humility, and submission to King Jesus.

At Hand or in the Future

So which is it—is the kingdom something available today, or is it that place we go after we die? A Hebraic way to answer this question is to say yes to both. The technical term for the future kingdom of God or second coming of Christ is the "*parousia*." When Daniel wrote of the coming kingdom, he couched it with language of the "Son of Man" (see Daniel 7). He said that on that day, all mankind would see "the abomination of desolation" as the "Son of Man" will suddenly separate the sheep from the goats through judgment (see Mathew 24). The wicked will be punished while the righteous finally experience the long-awaited peace of being kingdom citizens. Jesus speaks of the coming kingdom in Matthew 25:32–34:

> All the nations will be gathered before him, and he will separate them one from another, just as a shepherd separates the sheep from the goats. He will put the sheep on His right and the goats on the left. Then the King will say to those on His right, "Come, you who are blessed by my Father; inherit the kingdom prepared for you from the foundation of the world."

These things seem to point to a kingdom not-yet-come. But at the same time, we have to consider that Jesus' first message in Galilee announced that this kingdom was "at hand." It seems on the surface like an irreconcilable paradox.

If I polled one hundred Christians with the question, "When you think of the kingdom of heaven, do you think of a present reality to live in today or a place to enter into after death?," how would they respond? I think they would answer consistent with the way we've been preconditioned to believe in our western culture: heaven is a place we cross into after death.

What perpetuated this one-dimensional understanding of the kingdom can be traced to the notes section of the Scofield Bible. While many have benefited from the Scofield Bible, a future concept of the kingdom was taught in his commentary on Matthew 4 dealing with Jesus' message about the kingdom. In regards to the phrase, "at hand," Scofield notes:

> "At hand" is never a positive affirmation that the person or thing said to be "at hand" will immediately appear, but only that no known or predicted event must intervene. When Christ

appeared to the Jewish people, the next thing
in the order of revelation as it then stood,
should have been the setting up of the Davidic
kingdom. In the knowledge of God, not yet
disclosed, lay the rejection of the kingdom (and
King), the long period of the mystery-form of
the kingdom, the world-wide preaching of the
cross, and the out-calling of the Church. But
this was as yet locked up in the secret counsels
of God.[38]

Scofield had in mind a reality in which a King sets up an
earthly reign. Furthermore, his misconception of "at hand"
comes from looking at the word temporally, pertaining to time,
and not spatially, pertaining to existence. He interpreted the
phrase to imply something happening "soon." Since the Jews
rejected Christ and His message, the kingdom, therefore, was not
set up during His first coming, according to Scofield.

Other scholars believed Jesus came the first time to prepare
people for the future commencement of His kingdom upon His second arrival, notably Albert Schweitzer and Rudolf Bultmann. Both
viewed Jesus as an apocalyptic figure. What person in Jesus' day
held to this view? John the Baptist. So Jesus' response in Matthew
11, is His course-correction about his kingdom misconceptions.

Thinking with Two Hands

Modern, Western Christians have a hard time reconciling
how the kingdom can be both present and future. It may be useful for us, then, to adopt the method Jesus would've understood.
The Eastern culture processes these concepts by thinking with
two hands: on the one hand and on the other hand. Apparent

differences can both be correct simultaneously.[39] For Jesus, the emphasis of His teaching was on the imminence of the kingdom or its immediacy. He didn't only envision a future day when God's rule and reign would circumnavigate the Earth. "At hand" is a Hebraic colloquialism that can be interpreted spatially or temporally depending on the context.[40]

James uses the same word in two different ways. In James 4, he speaks of drawing near to God spatially as one would draw near to one's spouse:

> *Draw* near to God, and he will *draw* near to you. Cleanse your hands, sinners, and purify your hearts, you double-minded. (James 4:8)

He uses the word temporally in the following chapter:

> Therefore, brothers and sisters, be patient until the Lord's coming. See how the farmer waits for the precious fruit of the earth and is patient with it until it receives the early and the late rains. You also must be patient. Strengthen your hearts, because the Lord's coming is *near*. (James 5:7–8)

Sometimes Jesus refers to the coming kingdom of the Son of Man in the future as seen in Matthew 25, when He will separate the sheep from the goats, and in Mark: "And if your eye causes you to fall away, gouge it out. It is better for you to enter the kingdom of God with one eye than to have two eyes and be thrown into hell, where their worm does not die, and the fire is not quenched" (Mark 9:47–48).

Other times He speaks of the kingdom in the present as seen in Luke 17: "Being asked by the Pharisees when the kingdom of God would come, he answered them, 'The kingdom of God is not coming with something observable; no one will say, "See here!" or "There!" For you see, the kingdom of God is *in your midst*'" (Luke 17: 20–21).

You don't have to wait for the kingdom to come, as Jesus explains, for it's already here. Jesus is able to make this claim because its King has arrived. God's heavenly agenda is working in and through Him in the here and now as God's power breaks into the lives of people. His definition of the kingdom was very different than the kingdom the Jews were expecting, and we sometimes still make the same mistake, thinking of the kingdom in overly distant ways, different from how Jesus spoke of the kingdom. Will the kingdom come in all its fullness after the second coming of Christ? Yes. But it was inaugurated at Jesus' first coming.

Now and Then

George Eldon Ladd, former New Testament Professor at Fuller Theological Seminary, proposed a concept to balance the tension between Jesus' first and second coming in regards to setting up His kingdom. Using a term coined by Oscar Cullman, Ladd referred to "inaugurated eschatology,"[41] reasoning that Jesus' kingdom was *already* (initiated at His first coming), but *not yet* (realized fully at His second coming) simultaneously. He fused both concepts together while keeping them distinct. Pryor capitalizes on Ladd's work by replacing the "but" with "and" to propose: Jesus' kingdom is "already and so much more."[42] Our prayer, then, becomes, "God, break into our lives and world with greater power and authority. Save, heal, redeem, and rescue even more than you have done in times past. And do it today!"

When Jesus proclaims the words "at hand," He is simply saying that the kingdom is happening right now. D. T. Lancaster elaborates on the significance of this message: "Those who receive the forgiveness of their sins in this age and live by the rule of the kingdom (i.e., the Torah) in this present age can be said to have already laid hold of the kingdom of heaven, so to speak. [Rabbi Yechiel Tzvi] Liechtenstein describes the kingdom of heaven both as an external state when the Messiah reigns over the whole Earth and the internal state of the individual who is forgiven and spiritually regenerated by the Lord."[43] The future kingdom breaks into the lives of present day believers today.

One passage that has perpetuated a future-only perspective is found in the interrogation of Pilate. He asks Jesus point blank: "Are you the King of the Jews?" Jesus' response is, "My kingdom is not of this world. . . . If my kingdom were of this world, my servants would fight, so that I wouldn't be handed over to the Jews. But as it is, my kingdom is not from here" (John 18:36). We have taken the preposition "of" to mean "other-worldly," promoting an escapism mentality. However, the same preposition in Greek can be translated as "from," which connotes an entirely different meaning. Jesus is emphasizing quality, the kind of kingdom He offers, not destination, the location where the kingdom resides.

Is It God or Heaven?

An age-old debate is whether the kingdom of heaven is different than the kingdom of God. "Kingdom of God" is found sixty-eight times in ten different books of the New Testament compared to thirty-two occurrences of the phrase "kingdom of heaven." Interestingly, "kingdom of heaven" only occurs in

Matthew's Gospel. Some have suggested that the kingdom of God deals primarily with God working in the here and now, while "kingdom of heaven" refers to the future ruling of God in the afterlife. One author suggested, "The kingdom of God' is the 'reign of God' in the universe over all His created creatures, and includes time and eternity, heaven and earth. . . . 'The kingdom of heaven' is limited as to its time and its sphere. Its time is from the first to the second coming of Christ, and its sphere is over that part of the world that we call Christendom."[44]

Some view the kingdom in a similar way. Entering the kingdom is getting saved today, joining a church, and entering a realm the saints inherit when Christ returns to set up His kingship one day in the distant future. But all of these are shallow assumptions of what Jesus taught. Moreover, most of the sermons preached in pulpits around the world focus on ejecting from Earth to entering a heavenly amusement park one day. As a result, believers acquire a spiritual ticket at salvation and wait for their winning number to be called up yonder one day, sitting idly on the sidelines until Christ's return.

For Jesus, the "kingdom of God" and the "kingdom of heaven" are synonymous with each other. If you looked up *God*, in a Hebrew thesaurus, you would find *heaven* as an alternative. An example of this replacement is found in the parable of the prodigal son. Examining this familiar parable through a Hebraic lens is outside the scope of the book; however, I will make a few comments about the text. I've heard many messages focusing on the younger son or older brother, but the focal point of the story is the merciful father. When studying parables, it's important to uncover the one driving theme of the text. While there are subpoints along the way, Jesus has one truth He's attempting to communicate to His audience.

Reading the prodigal son parable separate from the other two parables in this section of Scripture misses the impact of the teaching. Jesus begins by describing a lost sheep in verse 3, a lost coin in verse 8, and then a lost son in verse 11. He moves His hearers from one hundred to ten to one. Hebrew is a language devoid of punctuation marks or emphasis tools like bold, italics, or underline. Instead of distinguishing points with punctuation or formatting, a Rabbi would employ repetition of words or progression of concepts. A careful observation of the text reveals another grammatical accentuation. Jesus starts with one sheep, moves to one silver coin, and ends with one son. He introduces with *animals*, moves to *inanimate objects*, and concludes with *human beings*, the crowing jewel of God's creation.

When Jesus finishes speaking, the audience is left asking themselves these questions: What kind of person leaves one hundred sheep to hunt for a lost one? God does. What kind of person searches high and low for one lost coin out of ten? God does. What kind of father forgives a son who humiliated him? God does.

Let's return to the prodigal son parable. When the son squanders his inheritance and comes to his senses in a pig farm, an untouchable, unclean animals, he devises a plan: "I'll get up, go to my father, and say to him, 'Father, I have sinned against heaven and in your sight'" (Luke 15:18). We can understand how the son can justify sinning against his father, but how can a person sin against heaven if it's only a place or realm? The logical answer is that he's referring to God. He recognized that accepting his inheritance prior to his death was a slap in the face of his heavenly father God. We use this word often even today when we say, "For heaven's sake" or "Heaven help us."

A New King Is in Town

Matthew describes something at the beginning of his Gospel that you may have missed if you weren't looking for it. In chapter 2, the title "king" is attached to Herod's name in Matthew 2:1, 2:3, and 2:9; however, it no longer appears after the magi (wise men) visit baby Jesus. Matthew has not forgotten Herod's title, but rather, is suggesting that, from this point on, Jesus is the true king of Israel. Matthew declares Jesus' identity at the outset of his letter. Herod may refer to himself with the title "king," but God is going to affirm His Son as the true king. The presentation of gifts from the wise men to baby Jesus are reminiscent of the time the Queen of Sheba brought gifts to King Solomon.[45]

> The queen of Sheba heard about Solomon's fame connected with the name of the LORD and came to test him with riddles. She came to Jerusalem with a very large entourage, with camels bearing spices, gold in great abundance, and precious stones. . . . Then she gave the king four and a half tons of gold, a great quantity of spices, and precious stones. Never again did such a quantity of spices arrive as those the queen of Sheba gave to King Solomon. (1 Kings 10:1–2, 10)

"Never again" has such a gift been given to a king until the birth of King Jesus when the magi "opened their treasures and presented him with gifts: gold, frankincense, and myrrh" (Matt. 2:11). All were gifts fit for a king.

Many scholars have meticulously parsed each Greek word of Matthew 28 and dissected each phrase for meaning, but few have uncovered the significance of the placement of this commission at the conclusion of Jesus' earthly ministry. Intending the commission as a crowning moment to His finished work, Jesus uses a play on words, communicating dual interpretations, by a single phrase to teach His followers about the establishment of His kingdom.

Jewish Sages taught their *talmidim* or disciples with *keshers*. Similar to hyperlinks on the Internet that connect one site to another, these connections are seen all throughout the Bible. We are often unable to identify them due to our lack of biblical knowledge, particularly our ignorance regarding the Old Testament. Without the use of chapters and verses, Rabbis would cue the minds of their audiences to a concept by only mentioning a phrase or a few words.

Our minds are well versed in this practice. For example, if I say, "Our Father," you might respond by saying, "who is in heaven. Hallowed be your name." What about this one: "Twas the night before Christmas"? Your response without thinking would be, "And all through the house." One lines brings to mind the rest of the poem. Jesus taught like this all the time.

The opening phrase, "All authority in heaven and on earth has been given to me," is a *kesher* or connection to Daniel 7:13–14, signifying the inauguration of the kingdom. Notice the kingdom language in that passage:

> Suddenly one like a son of man was coming with the clouds of heaven. He approached the Ancient of Days and was escorted before him. He was given *dominion,* and *glory,* and a *kingdom;* so that those of *every people, nation,* and *language* should serve him. *His dominion* is an *everlasting dominion* that will not pass away, and his kingdom is one that will not be destroyed.

Matthew has already identified Jesus as the "son of man" spoken of in Daniel's prophecy on two occasions (Matt. 24:30; 25:31). "Consequently, the command to 'make disciples of all nations' by 'teaching them to observe all that I have commanded you' (Matt. 28:19)," writes New Testament theologian G. K. Beale in his book *God Dwells Among Us*, "fulfills the prophecy that 'peoples, nations, and languages should serve' the son of man (Dan. 7:14)."[46] Moreover, "all nations" reverberates the promise made to Abraham in Genesis about God blessing all nations through his [Abraham's] seed (see Genesis 12).

Connecting the New to the Old

Another link in the Great Commission to the Old Testament is uncovered when we understand the order of the Old Testament books, what the Jews referred to as the TaNaK. The TaNaK is an acronym for the Old Testament books of the *Torah* (the first five books of the Bible: Genesis, Exodus, Leviticus, Numbers, and Deuteronomy), the *Nevi'im* (the books of the prophets beginning with the book of Joshua), and the *Ketuv'im* (the writings beginning with the book of Psalms). Our current Protestant Bibles contain the same books of the TaNaK with some alteration in how they are categorized. The final book of the TaNaK is not Malachi, as with our modern Bibles, but rather 2 Chronicles. Interestingly, the Hebrew Bible doesn't end with the silence of the final prophet Malachi but with a commission to reconstruct the Temple. Locate the similarities between the final verse in 2 Chronicles and the final commission of Jesus in the Great Commission:

> In the first year of King Cyrus of Persia, in order to fulfill the word of the LORD spoken

through Jeremiah, the LORD roused the spirit of King Cyrus of Persia to issue a proclamation throughout his entire kingdom and also to put it in writing: This is what King Cyrus of Persia says: The LORD, the God of the heavens, has given me all the kingdoms of the earth and has appointed me to build him a Temple at Jerusalem in Judah. Any of his people among you may go up, and may the LORD his God be with him. (2 Chron. 36:22–23)

Jesus came near and said to them, "All authority has been given to me in heaven and on earth. Go, therefore, and make disciples of all nations, baptizing them in the name of the Father and of the Son and of the Holy Spirit, teaching them to observe everything I have commanded you. And remember, I am with you always, to the end of the age." (Matt. 28:18–20)

G. K. Beale sees three connections between the two passages:

(1) Both Cyrus and Jesus assert authority over all the earth, (2) the commission to "go," and (3) the assurance of the divine presence to fulfill the commission ["I will be with you always"]. By alluding to the last verse of the Hebrew Bible (2 Chron. 36:23) at the conclusion of this Gospel, Matthew seems to construct his Gospel on the framework of 1 and 2 Chronicles. . . . Just as 1 Chronicles begins with an extensive genealogy of the kings of Israel, so Matthew begins with the genealogy of King

Jesus, in partial dependence on 1 Chronicles 1–3. Just as 2 Chronicles ends with the Temple-building commission of the "messiah" Cyrus (see Isa. 44:28–45:1), so Matthew ends with the Temple-building commission of the Messiah Jesus (Matt. 28:19). . . . In this respect, the 2 Chronicles passage would be viewed as a historical event commissioning a Temple that foreshadowed typologically the much greater event of Jesus' Great Commission to build a greater.[47]

This is exactly why Paul can say to the believers in Corinth, "Don't you yourselves know that you are God's temple and that the Spirit of God lives in you?" (1 Cor. 3:16). Unlike earthly kings who will come and go, we have a heavenly King who remains with us forever. Matthew's Gospel can be framed around the premise "How God became King."[48]

This King is not some distant ruler, living above and beyond His creation. No. His desire is to be with His people. Matthew organizes his Gospel around this concept by bracketing the entire book to communicate the importance of God with us. The final line of Matthew, "And remember, I am with you always, to the end of the age," connects the end of the book to the beginning. "I am with you" in Hebrew is one word, "Immanuel."

The first few verses of Matthew's Gospel chronicle the angelic encounter with Joseph, Jesus' earthly father. Matthew does the heavy lifting for the reader by connecting the dots of this prophecy from Isaiah: "See, the virgin will become pregnant and give birth to a son, and they will name him *Immanuel*, which is translated, '*God is with us.*'" At the outset, Matthew is communicating the imminence of God with His people, and at the conclusion, he leaves his audience with the same promise.

CHAPTER 6

The Kingdom Has Come

The Bible begins with a marriage in Genesis and ends with a wedding ceremony in Revelation 21 and 22. As explained earlier, a marriage covenant is a visual picture of the gospel and the kingdom. When we reduce the Christian life simply to leaving Earth to live in heaven, we miss the glorious end of God's consummation of all things. The God who created heaven and Earth in the beginning is going to renew and restore it in the end. God will not discard the old canvas in place of a new one. Rather, He will renew the existing one. The marriage picture, the joining of husband and wife on Earth, and in this case Jesus Christ and His church, changes our perspective of the last days and the purpose of life today. As symbols of heaven on Earth, our actions today have a deeper meaning to them, knowing that one day God will make all wrongs right and renew His creation on Earth.

Jesus' arrival signifies God's plan kicking into action. By embodying the tabernacle/Temple of the Old Testament, He proves He's the King of God's kingdom from centuries before. Beale writes,

> On him, not on the Temple, rests the "Shekinah"
> glory in an even greater way than previously in

the temple. Therefore, Jesus not only takes over the Temple's role in sacrifice, but becomes the unique place for God's special revelatory presence. God began to manifest His glorious presence in Jesus' life, death and resurrection in a greater way than it was ever manifested in Israel's old, physical Temple structure.[49]

The kingdom of heaven consumed His thoughts and monopolized the messages He preached. Surprisingly, the word *church* (*ekklesia*) is used only three times in the Gospels (Matt. 16:18; Matt. 18:17). The phrase kingdom of God, by comparison, is found forty-one times and the phrase kingdom of heaven (in Matthew's Gospel alone) is found thirty-one times.

It's no surprise what the topic of Jesus' first formal message after John was arrested is about. You guessed it: "The time is fulfilled, and the *kingdom of God* has come near. Repent and believe the good news!" (Mark 1:15). His final conversation with the disciples before ascending to heaven is about the same thing:

> So when they had come together, they asked him, "Lord, are you restoring the *kingdom* to Israel at this time?" He said to them, "It is not for you to know times or periods that the Father has set by his own authority. But you will receive power when the Holy Spirit has come on you, and you will be my witnesses in Jerusalem, in all Judea and Samaria, and to the end of the earth." (Acts 1:6–8)

The book of Acts closes with a synopsis of Paul's preaching. Concurrent with Christ's emphasis, Paul, from "dawn to dusk, expounded and testified about the *kingdom of God*. He tried to persuade them about Jesus from both the Law of Moses and the Prophets" (Acts 28:23). A few verses down, Acts concludes: "Paul stayed two whole years in his own rented house. And he welcomed all who visited him, proclaiming the *kingdom of God* and teaching about the Lord Jesus Christ with all boldness and without hindrance" (Acts 28:30–31). The kingdom permeated every message both Jesus and Paul proclaimed. Unfortunately, the same can't be said of modern preaching today. Before I throw anyone else under the bus, I want to include my own sermons in the equation. How many sermons have you heard on the kingdom of heaven? How many messages have you listened to on how to live in the kingdom today? I have a sneaking suspicion the number can be counted on one hand. We've heard countless sermons on Jesus, but Jesus was always preaching about the kingdom. I understand that Jesus and the kingdom are inseparable, but the point I am making is that our focus is different than Jesus' was.

Possibly, our understanding of the kingdom, or lack thereof, may be the result of the sparse sermons we've heard or few messages we've preached. A proper understanding, I believe, will lead to more sermons about the most important agenda item on Jesus' earthly to-do list. Before we define what the kingdom is, we need to determine when and how it arrived. Thankfully for us, Jesus pinpoints its inauguration with John the Baptist's ministry.

For modern Christians, we hear about the kingdom of heaven and think of the future. For Jesus, the vast majority of time He speaks of the kingdom in the present. Malcolm Muggeridge said, "Jesus' good news, then, was that the kingdom of God had come, and that he, Jesus, was its herald and expounder to men. More than that, in some special, mysterious way, he was the kingdom."[50]

Entering the Kingdom: Faith and Repentance

Kingdom citizenship is limited to those who follow the king. While God is providential king over the Earth ("Heaven is my throne, and earth is my footstool" (Isa. 66:1), only those who enter and submit to His rule experience His rewards. Believers enter the kingdom at the moment of salvation. D. A. Carson suggests that John 5:24, "Anyone who hears my word and believes him who sent me has eternal life and will not come under judgment but has passed from death to life," provides the "strongest affirmation of inaugurated eschatology [the present kingdom] in the fourth Gospel. . . . [We do not need to] wait until the last day to experience something of resurrection life."[51] Paul's promise of resurrection power to the Ephesian believers makes sense in light of this statement. He prayed for believers to know the "mighty working of his strength" seen "in Christ by [God] raising him from the dead and seating him at his right hand in the heavens" (Eph. 1:19–20).

Jesus offered Nicodemus a similar invitation to enter the kingdom "today" in John 3. In hopes of avoiding attention being drawn to himself, Nicodemus finds Jesus at night. The mention of the time of day is a metaphor for something greater than the placement of the sun and moon. John uses the contrast of light and darkness to reveal the spiritual condition of people in his Gospel (see John 1:5; 3:2; 3:19; 9:4–5; 12:35; and 20:1). Nicodemus, as the representative of the nation of Israel, was searching in the darkness for Jesus in more ways than one. Jesus directs him to the pathway for entering the kingdom: "you must be born again" (John 3:3). Jesus, by speaking this way, rejects the notion that Jews were granted entrance into the kingdom by birth and proposes a two-fold birth and rebirth through both water (renewal) and spirit (cleansing).[52] Unless a person is washed and renewed through the Word and by the Holy Spirit, he or she cannot enter God's kingdom. Jesus eliminates meritorious works from the salvation equation.

Eternal life and entering the kingdom are one and the same. The rich young ruler asked, "What must I do to inherit eternal life?" As he is walking away, Jesus states, "It is hard for a rich person to enter the kingdom of God." In John 17, Jesus speaks of eternal life today: "This is eternal life: that they may know you, the only true God, and the one you have sent—Jesus Christ" (John 17:3). Knowing, in this context, is a personal, interactive relationship with another person, similar to the intimacy shared between a husband and wife (see Gen. 4:1).

Dallas Willard, in his work *The Divine Conspiracy*, suggests, "When he [Jesus] announced that the 'governance' or rule of God had become available to human beings, he was primarily referring to what he could do for people, God acting with him. But he was also offering to communicate this same 'rule of God' to others who would receive and learn it from him. He was himself the evidence for the truth of his announcement about the availability of God's kingdom, or governance, to ordinary human existence."[53] In order for this shift to happen in our lives, we need to adopt a kingdom vocabulary.

Language Changes Culture

The biggest news in American on July 22, 2013, had nothing to do with anything on this side of the pond. News cameras, TV reporters, and Internet sites were buzzing with excitement as Prince William, Duke of Cambridge, and Catherine "Kate," Duchess of Cambridge, gave birth to their first son Prince George. Although a monarchy is foreign to Americans, many are enamored with the royal couple of England. The entire system is built upon loyalty, respect, and submission to leadership. Unlike the democracy in which we reside, citizens in traditional monarchies are "subject" to the rule of a king or queen who assumes the representational duties set in place over thousands of years. Citizens subject themselves willingly to the rule of their leader and in return enjoy the blessings afforded by being a kingdom citizen.

"Subjects," as these residents are called, has altogether become a lost word in our western world. However, this concept will be helpful in our understanding of Jesus' kingdom. A "subject" has multiple roles as a kingdom citizen, not the least of which is representing the crown everywhere they go. Each person is an image bearer or witness to the monarchy, and with great privilege comes great responsibility.

Similarly, Jesus envisioned this citizenry when He pronounced the kingdom has come. The kingdom message seasoned His sermons. The Gospel writers went to great lengths to ensure their readers understood this truth.

The First Sermon

Every preacher can recall his first sermon. Mine, needless to say, was not one of my best. I'm thankful that YouTube and Vimeo didn't exist back then. I invested three weeks of working, examining, and interpreting Luke 23:39–42 on Jesus being crucified between two thieves on the cross. My audience consisted of fifty to sixty men and women waiting to eat supper at the Brantley Center, a faith-based homeless shelter in New Orleans. Most in the audience were underwhelmed to be there since chapel attendance was mandatory in order to receive a hot meal. With palms sweating from excitement, I rocked back and forth behind the makeshift pulpit, a tilted music stand, as I delivered my first message. Although the night was memorable, the sermon was mediocre.

Let's journey to listen to the first recorded public message of Jesus in Mark 1. Think of the most polished communicator you've ever heard. They fade in comparison to the greatest orator ever to walk planet Earth. As the walking Word of God, Jesus' preaching was unlike anything anyone had ever heard before. The religious leaders even noted that "he was teaching them as one who had authority, and not like the scribes" (Mark 1:21–22). Jesus was not merely piggybacking on the authority of others; He Himself was the authority. Truth spoken by His lips penetrated the ears and pricked the hearts He formed by hand.

Jesus personified perfection, excellence, and eloquence. Commentator and pastor, R. Kent Hughes, describes His presentation:

> His [Jesus] *logos*, his word, was perfect. Whatever he said was absolutely true. His exegesis of Scripture was flawless. His application of spiritual truth was the most penetrating in all of history, as we see in such discourses as the Sermon on the Mount. His *ethos*, the kind of person he was, was without parallel in the human race. The tone of his voice, the expression on his face, the integrity of his eyes flowed with truth. His *pathos* came from a heart absolutely convinced of man's need, absolutely loving, and absolutely determined. There never has been anyone as truly passionate as Christ in all human experience. These three, his *logos*, *ethos*, and *pathos*, blended in Christ with such ineluctable force

that he, from the beginning, was the greatest communicator the world has ever known![54]

His initial message proclaimed the inauguration of the kingdom: "The time is fulfilled, and the kingdom of God has come near. Repent and believe the good news!" (Mark 1:15). This was hardly a one-time message. After departing from a quiet place of prayer one morning, He unfolded His mission to the early disciples: "It is necessary for me to proclaim the good news about the *kingdom of God* to the other towns also, because I was sent for this purpose" (Luke 4:43).

A Person, Power, and People

Simply put, the kingdom of heaven is the rule and reign of God over one's life. C. S. Song, in his book *Jesus and the Reign of God*, describes the concept:

> To know what Jesus means by abundant life, one must know what he means by the reign of God. To experience abundant life, one must know what he means by the reign of God. To experience that life, one must experience God's reign. To live that life, one must live God's reign in one's own life. The scope of God's reign determines the scope of Jesus' life and work. Its vision is Jesus' vision. Its goal is Jesus' goal. Is not, then, to know Jesus to know God's reign? The abundant life that comes from God's reign is very different from the life of affluence enjoyed by those with plenty of material means.[55]

For Jesus, the kingdom is multi-dimensional in its scope and significance. Pryor identifies three primary ways that Jesus used the phrase: "The kingdom draws attention to a person. The kingdom emphasizes a power presently at work. The kingdom refers collectively to a people who have entered it as followers of Jesus."[56]

Kingdom as a Person

Jesus oftentimes spoke of the kingdom being near (spatially) to those around Him. When a Pharisee questioned Him about the kingdom in Luke 17, He responded by saying, "The kingdom of God is not coming with something observable; no one will say, 'See here!' or 'There!' For you see, the kingdom of God is in your midst" (Luke 17:20–21). The audience would have deduced that a king was among them for a kingdom to be present. Jesus is exclaiming, "I'm here! Your long-awaited King has arrived. The one you've longed for is on the scene." Referring to the kingdom in this manner is always indicative of a king's arrival. You may be wondering why Jesus didn't just come out and disclose His identity. It was not customary in Eastern culture for a person to boast about his identity. A good Rabbi would pull these insights out of his hearers.

When the High Priest Caiaphas demanded, "I charge you under oath by the living God: Tell us if you are the Messiah, the Son of God." Jesus replied, "You have said it" (Matt 26:63–64). Later that night Pilate asked Jesus the same question, "Are you the king of the Jews?" Jesus responded the same way: "You say so" (Luke 23:3).

God even used a Roman leader to identify Jesus to those witnessing the crucifixion by making a placard for the cross with the title: "Jesus of Nazareth, the King of the Jews" (John 19:19).

Don't miss the following sentence: "Many of the Jews read this sign, because the place where Jesus was crucified was near the city, and it was written in *Aramaic, Latin,* and *Greek*" (John 19:20). Pilate inscribes these lines in three languages into the wooden sign above the head of Jesus to remove any shadow of doubt who He is and what He came to do.

On one occasion, Jesus takes His disciples on a twenty-eight mile field trip to Caesarea Philippi for their midterm exam. On the edge of Mount Hermon was a cave that flowed with water from a huge hole in the Earth. Pagan worshippers believed this cave or gate was the entranceway to Hades or the underworld. The main form of worship was of the false god Pan, a half-man/half-goat being. Prostitution and lewd sexual acts were commonplace in association with Pan worship.

Another form of worship that was commonplace in this region was emperor worship. Imagine walking on Bourbon Street on Fat Tuesday or Mardi Gras day. Better yet, don't imagine that. I think you get the point.

The exam is simple, only two questions: Who do people say that the Son of Man is? Who do you say that I am? (Matt. 16:13, 15). Surrounded by false deities claiming to be the true God, Peter declares, "You are the Messiah, the Son of the living God" (Matt. 16:16). Notice, he adds "living" God to discount the substandard imitations surrounding them. It is worth noting that the Jewish people used the word *Messiah* synonymously for king during the time of Jesus.[57]

Jesus, then, makes a declaration about the kingdom in connection with His identity as the Messiah: "And I also say to you that you are Peter, and on this rock I will build my church, and the gates of Hades will not overpower it. I will give you the keys of the kingdom of heaven, and whatever you bind on earth will have been bound in heaven, and whatever you loose on earth will have been loosed in heaven" (Matt. 16:18–19). Because He is the ruling and reigning King, His disciples are able to advance in battle against the enemy. Ray Vander Laan notes that the cave of Pan was referred to as a gate to the underworld in the first century.[58] Kingdoms used gates as protection in the ancient world. By Jesus stating, "The gates of Hades will not overpower or prevail," He was presenting a challenge to His disciples.

In the first century, Rabbis would give a key to a disciple who mastered their teachings, similar to a graduation certificate. The key bore the insignia of the mentor. For example, a person who possessed Gamaliel's key, Paul's mentor, embodied his life and teaching. The disciple moved beyond just understanding what the Rabbi taught to emulating how he lived. A Rabbinic commentary on the Talmud notes: "These keys were put into the hands of the Sages' disciples who had received the [interpretations of hidden wisdom] from their teachers, and [the Sages] relied upon them to transmit this wisdom only to those among their disciples who were as worthy as they themselves."[59] G. Campbell Morgan concurs with this idea of passing keys to disciples who understood important concepts. He states, "The keys of the Kingdom were given to the illuminated, to those who understood the principle of the kingdom, the laws of the Kingdom, [and] the method of the kingdom."[60]

The kingdom of heaven expands, not through passivity, but advancement. This was no time for sitting around waiting for the return of Christ. The days of hiding inside while evil prevails outside are over. They were to be change agents in a corrupt world by standing against evil. Jesus' half brother James encapsulates this truth in his epistle: "Therefore, submit to God. *Resist* the devil, and he will flee from you" (James 4:7). When you submit to the king of the kingdom, you will be able to stand against the devil. Remember Paul's words to the Ephesians: "For this reason take up the full armor of God, so that you may be able to *resist* in the evil day, and having prepared everything, to take your stand" (Eph. 6:13).

Kingdom as a Power

In addition to referencing the kingdom as a person, Jesus speaks of His movement as a power. It's God's power working through His people. Paul exclaimed, "For the kingdom of God is not a matter of talk but of *power*" (1 Cor. 4:20). Our Western minds are stretched to understand this concept. An example in English would be "Running is fun." The noun is formed from the verb *run*. In this category, "kingdom" is used as a verbal noun to describe God's activity in the world. We should not think of it as God's kingdom *in* heaven, but the kingdom *of* heaven.

In the person of Jesus, God has intersected space and time to carry out His heavenly agenda. Jesus follows up physical healings with the explanation, "The kingdom of God has come upon you" (Luke 10:9). When His authority is questioned by the religious leaders, He responds: "If I drive out demons by the finger of God, then the kingdom of God has come upon you" (Luke 11:20). The phrase "finger of God" is a reference to God's power displayed in Exodus 31:18 when God wrote the words of the covenant, the Ten Commandments, by His own finger or power.

The seventy disciples are sent out in Luke 10 with instructions from Jesus: "When you enter any town, and they welcome you, eat the things set before you. Heal the sick who are there, and tell them, 'The kingdom of God has come near you'" (Luke 10:8-9).[61] The everlasting authority of God is now realized in the person of Jesus. The process is always the same: God redeems to reveal Himself to us in order to reign over us (the Passover/ Pentecost paradigm). Our response is to live responsibly by the commands of God. We don't observe Christ's commands out of duty but out of devotion.

Kingdom as a People

The kingdom is also used to identify the citizens who live under the rule and reign of King Jesus through responding to the commands of the King and thereby experiencing the benefits of the kingdom. When a rich younger ruler inquired about how to inherit eternal life (enter the kingdom), Jesus questions him about obedience to the Old Testament commandments to which he responds in the affirmative. Jesus gets to the heart of the problem which is a problem of his heart: "You still lack one thing: Sell all you have and distribute it to the poor, and you will have treasure in heaven. Then come, follow me" (Luke 18:22). Jesus, then, extends an offer to join His movement as a kingdom resident. What follows is the saddest verse, in my opinion, in the Gospels: "After he heard this, he became extremely sad, because he was very rich" (Luke 18:23). We witness someone in arm's reach of salvation rejecting the offer of Jesus.

"Jesus, what are you doing? This man has enough assets to bankroll our fledgling ministry. Why don't you make a deal with the man?" Some health, wealth, and prosperity preachers would have capitalized on this man's capital. "I didn't mean sell it all. How about sell half? How about 50 cents on the dollar?" These words are never uttered from the mouth of Jesus. Neither does Jesus say, "Sell it all and give the money to *me*."

The rich younger ruler is forbidden from entering the kingdom because of his adherence to money. As he walks away, Jesus turns to His disciples and says, "How hard it is for those who have wealth to enter the kingdom of God! For it is easier for a camel to go through the eye of a needle than for a rich person to enter the kingdom of God" (Luke 18:24–25). I've heard preachers expound this verse one-dimensionally as only a future prohibition. (Sadly, I'm guilty when it comes to doing this as well in years past.) The key to interpreting this encounter is the tense of the word *enter*. The present tense aspect promises a realization today. Jesus is not excluding rich people from entering heaven after they die; He is warning against missing out on the blessings and the benefits of the kingdom of heaven *today* because of the distraction of serving money. "You can't serve both God and money." Divided loyalties are non-existent in His kingdom. To be a subject in the kingdom of heaven demands militant loyalty to the king. The young man withdraws his name from the roster in the movement of King Jesus.

Moreover, entrance into the kingdom movement is found at the conclusion of the Sermon on the Mount in Matthew 7. Jesus warns against "word only" allegiance. "Not everyone who says to me, 'Lord, Lord,' will enter the kingdom of heaven [his movement], but only the one who does the will of my Father in heaven" (Matt. 7:21). Entrance is through grace by faith in Christ, but blessings come through obedience to Christ. Our works are not an initiation into the kingdom. They are a demonstration of our participation.

Another occurrence of people as the kingdom of heaven is seen at the end of another one of Jesus' parables: "What do you think? A man had two sons. He went to the first and said, 'My son, go work in the vineyard today.' "He answered, 'I don't want to,' but later he changed his mind and went. Then the man went to the other and said the same thing. 'I will, sir,' he answered, but he didn't go. Which of the two did his father's will?" They said,

"The first." Jesus said to them, "Truly I tell you, tax collectors and prostitutes are entering the kingdom of God before you. For John came to you in the way of righteousness, and you didn't believe him. Tax collectors and prostitutes did believe him; but you, when you saw it, didn't even change your minds then and believe him" (Matt. 21:28–32).

If you haven't noticed by now, the kingdom is rarely used to denote a place to go after death. The overwhelming majority of time it's a here-and-now reality or power in someone's life today. Dallas Willard supports this idea:

> The reality of God's rule, and all of the instru-
> mentalities it involves, is present in action and
> available with and through the person of Jesus.
> That is Jesus' Gospel. The obvious present reality
> of the kingdom is what provoked the responses
> we have just discussed. New Testament passages
> make plain that this kingdom is not something
> to be "accepted" now and enjoyed later, but
> something to be entered now.[62]

The Gospels repeatedly emphasize the importance of being alive today and not waiting for tomorrow.

No Place Like Home

Isaiah prophesied about the Messiah's coming seven hundred years before His arrival: "The Spirit of the Lord God is upon me, because the Lord has anointed me to bring good news to the poor; he has sent me to bind up the brokenhearted, to proclaim liberty to the captives, and the opening of the prison to those who are bound; to proclaim the year of the Lord's favor, and the day of vengeance of our God; to comfort all who mourn" (Isa. 61:1–2 ESV). Every Jewish boy and girl could recite Isaiah 61 by memory, especially in Nazareth. Residents believed the Messiah would come from their hometown because of the reference in Isaiah: "There shall come forth a shoot from the stump of Jesse, and a branch from his roots shall bear fruit."

The Hebrew word for *shoot* is *netzer;* we get the English word *Nazareth* from this word. Rabbi Lichtenstein connects the two words: "All the prophets said that Messiah's name is *tzemach*, 'Branch' (Zech. 3:8; 6:12; Jeremiah 23:5; and Isaiah 4:2). Isaiah also called him *netzer* in 11:1, since *netzer* and *tzemach* are synonyms. This hints at the name Yeshua the Nazarene (*notzri*) and that he would be called a notzri."[63] The town was bursting with nationalistic zeal for Israel.

Bible teacher Ray Vander Laan proposes that at the time of Jesus the people of Nazareth may have affectionately referred to their town in a way we would translate as "shootville" or "branchtown."[64] Since the throne of David hadn't been occupied for more than five hundred years, the city became a breeding ground for insurrectionist activity as the fanatical citizens perpetuated the idea the Messiah would come from Nazareth.

On one occasion, Jesus was asked to deliver the message at His hometown synagogue after launching His earthly ministry. He hadn't officially called the Twelve yet, so He probably traveled with five disciples that day (John, Andrew, Peter, James, and Matthew). Since Nazareth was a small town of only two hundred inhabitants, many of Jesus' uncles, aunts, cousins, nephews, nieces, brothers, and sisters would have been in attendance at the synagogue that day. Imagine the scene as the disciples paraded into the synagogue behind their Rabbi. Anticipation was palpable that morning, as onlookers wondered: "Could Jesus be the long-awaited Messiah?"

The service began with the public reading of Scripture for around forty minutes while the people stood in worship. "As was his custom, [Jesus] went to the synagogue on the Sabbath day, and he stood up to read," Luke 4:16 (ESV) tells us. He implies that Jesus had been doing this often. Following the pattern of the service, Jesus began with a reading from the Torah. We read in Luke 4:16 that, as usual, He entered the synagogue on the Sabbath day and stood up to read the Torah. Then, He followed His reading of the Torah with a reading from the Prophets. Luke 4:17–19 says:

> The scroll of the prophet Isaiah was given to him, and unrolling the scroll, he found the place where it was written: "The Spirit of the Lord is on me, because he has anointed me to preach good news to the poor. He has sent me to proclaim release to the captives and recovery of sight to the blind, to set free the oppressed, to proclaim the year of the Lord's favor."

Jesus demonstrates a common rabbinical technique called "stringing pearls," where He connects multiple passages of Scripture together to prove a point.[65] "Pearls" is an image that was synonymous with Scripture, as used by Jesus in Matthew 7:6 when He warns against casting pearls before swine. In this case, Jesus reads from Isaiah 61:1–2 and strings a pearl by inserting a line from Isaiah 58:6, "to set the oppressed free." Amazingly, He links together the only two passages in the Old Testament that refer to the favor of the Lord (Isa. 58:5 and 61:2).[66] By making this connection, Jesus provides "two witnesses to his main message and thereby emphasizes to his listeners that the proclamation of the 'favor of the Lord' will be at the heart of his ministry as the Messiah."[67]

The audience is on the edge of their stone seats waiting to hear Jesus' interpretation of this messianic text. Jesus "rolled up the scroll, gave it back to the attendant, and sat down. And the eyes of everyone in the synagogue were fixed on him" (Luke 4:20). With every eye upon Him, Jesus delivered the shortest sermon ever delivered by a Rabbi: "Today as you listen, this Scripture has been fulfilled" (v. 21). It's quite clear what He is proposing: "I am the promised Messiah." It's difficult for our modern minds to grasp the impact of Jesus' words that day. The nation has been retelling the story of God's coming literally hundreds and hundreds of years. And now it was happening before their eyes.

Jubilee Is Here

But Jesus, you left one line out. It was that one phrase they longed to see come to fruition: "the day of vengeance of our God" (Isa. 61:2b KJV). At that time, God would pummel their enemies for years of turmoil by setting up His kingdom led by the Messiah, and as a result, the people would finally be set free.

The "favor of the Lord" or the Jubilee was a celebratory time every half century where debts would be forgiven, things would be put right, slaves would be freed, and property would be returned. The nation looked forward to this time when they could start over again. Notice how the people respond in verse 22: "They were all speaking well of him and were amazed by the gracious words that came from his mouth; yet they said, 'Isn't this Joseph's son?'" (Luke 4:22).

The people were not questioning Jesus' claims; they were affirming His identity as Joseph's son. Everyone in the town knew that Joseph was of the lineage of David, a shoot of Jesse, and that Jesus was His son. Jesus, however, knew that these people were looking to Him for their own personal gain. The people had built up in their minds a picture of what the Messiah would be like according to their own expectations, and they would not be able to accept what He had come to do.

Discerning the town was boiling over with vengeance not liberation, Jesus squelched their expectancy. He announced, "No prophet is accepted in his hometown" (Luke 4:24), before referencing two Old Testament passages where God overlooked the Jewish people to extend healing and assistance to Gentiles. His message was clear. In the same way Elijah bypassed Israel to care for a Gentile woman and Elisha healed a Gentile leper instead of an Israelite leper, Jesus was about to redirect His messianic ministry outside of Nazareth. The mood turned quickly sour as the townspeople attempted to throw Him off a cliff. Ironically, the townspeople who wanted the peace of God for Israel responded to Jesus with vengeance and anger.

As Jesus shook the dust off His feet before leaving town, His message reverberated in the minds of His hometown neighbors: the long anticipated kingdom of God has commenced. Now, Jesus will devote the remainder of His ministry to raising up men who will continue spreading the good news of the kingdom long after He ascended to heaven.

CHAPTER 7

In the World, but Not of the World

We've already seen how Jesus speaks throughout the Gospels of the kingdom in three spheres: a person, a place, and a power. Most often, He referred to the kingdom as a present power that is ruling over one's life, not in terms of a future place to wait for until after we die. A citizen of the kingdom follows the instructions of the king, a response that garners blessings, favor, and abundant life today. It's difficult for our minds to comprehend the future kingdom breaking into our present-day lives, since most have taught to think one-dimensional in the sense of heaven coming tomorrow while we wait today. As stated in the previous chapter, we must think on two hands or with a both/and not an either/or mentality. An example to help us comprehend this perceived paradox is the way we purchase homes. How many of you own a home or have parents who own their own homes? Many of you would affirm that you own your home and don't rent it. After moving in you decorated it the way you wanted, drove nails in the wall, hung pictures in the hallway, painted some walls, and laid flooring in certain rooms.

You hired a plumber to fix the toilet when it broke and hired a Heating and Air company to fix the A/C when it went out. You pay taxes and insurance on your home. It's your home. But do you really own it?[68]

The bank actually owns your home until the mortgage is paid off. Technically, you own it, but you won't realize it fully until it's paid in full. We live in the kingdom now but will experience it fully when Christ returns. When we apply this present kingdom hermeneutic to parables and encounters, we will understand our role in the kingdom. "The kingdom of God," according to author Reggie McNeal, "is life as God intends it to be, his original blueprint for all of creation."[69] Let's gaze through a present perspective at familiar passages on the kingdom of heaven.

Concealing the Secrets of the Kingdom

The first kingdom parable is found after a major shift in Jesus' ministry. After the religious leaders label His movement of demonic origins, Jesus turns His attention to the disciples who are following Him. The nation, as Jesus indicates, has committed the unpardonable sin, rejecting Jesus as the only means by which they can be saved, therefore, prompting Jesus to turn His attention solely to raising up His disciples by teaching through parables, fulfilling what the psalmist said in Psalm 78:2 (NIV): "I will open my mouth with a parable; I will utter hidden things, things from of old."

Matthew records Jesus' reason for teaching in parables: "Then the disciples came and said to him, 'Why do you speak to them in parables?' And he answered them, 'To you it has been given to know the secrets of the kingdom of heaven, but to them it has not been given'" (Matt. 13:10–11 ESV). New

Testament scholar Richard Hays supports this shift in Jesus' teaching to intentionally conceal His message from this point on: "His [Jesus] teaching in parables produces a concealment of his message."[70] What He conceals to the crowd, He reveals to His disciples.

Krister Stendahl accentuates the importance of this kingdom teaching: "Of all the some hundred themes that he [Jesus] could have lifted up from the Jewish tradition . . . and of all the infinite number of themes available to him in his divine fullness, he chose this one: the kingdom."[71] The sower and the seed parable describes those who enter the kingdom and those who live outside the kingdom on Earth today. The goal of the seed is to produce fruit, which is a God-honoring life of service to God. He's not talking about growing a garden. He's talking about obedience to the king as a citizen of the kingdom in response to His message.

I've interpreted this parable through the years as describing three unbelieving soils (sown on the path, rocky ground, and thorns) versus one believing soil (good ground). Most would affirm this interpretation of the text. I began asking myself the hard question: If this is the case, only a small percentage of people are truly saved? While the passage explains how people respond to our message, the meaning is deeper. Jesus' explanation of the passage sheds light on its meaning.

> So listen to the parable of the sower: When anyone hears the word about the kingdom and doesn't understand it, the evil one comes and snatches away what was sown in his heart. This is the one sown along the path. And the one sown on rocky ground—this is one who hears the word and immediately receives it with joy. But he has no root and is short-lived. When

> distress or persecution comes because of the word, immediately he falls away. Now the one sown among the thorns—this is one who hears the word, but the worries of this age and the deceitfulness of wealth choke the word, and it becomes unfruitful. But the one sown on the good ground—this is one who hears and understands the word, who does produce fruit and yields: some a hundred, some sixty, some thirty times what was sown. (Matt. 13:18–23)

The parable is about "hearing" the Word of God and doing it. Jesus' words are not an evangelistic plea for lost people to be saved but a guidebook for diagnosing who is and isn't saved. But "hearing" in the first century is monumentally different than how we hear today. Hearing is not just listening to something that is spoken, but acting upon what is heard. The connection between hearing and obeying is seen in Deuteronomy 4: "And now, O Israel, listen to the statutes and the rules that I am teaching you, and do them, that you may live, and go in and take possession of the land that the LORD, the God of your fathers, is giving you" (Deut. 4:1 ESV). Again, in Deuteronomy 5:1, we notice the connection between hearing and doing: "Hear, O Israel, the statutes and the rules that I speak in your hearing today, and you shall learn them and be careful to do them" (ESV).

When I was a child, my mother would instruct my sister and me to pick up our toys before bed. Five minutes later she would enter my bedroom to find the toys exactly where they lay before. She would speak louder this time: "Clean up your room before bed. You have school tomorrow." A few minutes later, she would enter again to find—you guessed it—the toys unmoved. "Robby," she would say, "did you *hear* what I said?" I heard her loud and clear. Who couldn't hear a mom's voice spoken to an unresponsive son? However, she wasn't interested in whether I heard her or not. She wanted me to do something about it. Similarly, the sower parable is about obedience that leads to maturity.

We all know people who have made a supposed "profession of faith" in Christ, but have not surrendered their lives to Christ. They are not seeking first the kingdom daily; they are not dying to self daily; they are not carrying their cross, and they are not taking on Jesus' yoke, and as a result they are no longer walking with the Lord.

Not only did Jesus teach through visual examples of sowers, gardeners, and fishermen, but He also used human illustrations to communicate His messages. A second soil example could be found in John: "When many of his disciples heard it, they said, 'This is a hard saying; who can listen to it?' . . . After this many of his disciples turned back and no longer walked with him" (John 6:60, 66 ESV). Rejection of Jesus' words becomes the impediment for seed taking root and producing fruit.

The rich young ruler would be an example of a third soil heart, someone who missed living in the kingdom today by rejecting the words of Jesus for temporal riches. "As for what was sown among thorns, this is the one who hears the word, but the cares of the world and the deceitfulness of riches choke the word, and it proves unfruitful" (Matt. 13:22 ESV). Further evidence is seen in Jesus' discussion about money in the Sermon on the Mount: "No one can serve two masters, for either he will hate the one and love the other, or he will be devoted to the one and despise the other. You cannot serve God and money" (Matt. 6:24 ESV). Jesus doesn't preclude rich men from entering heaven. Through Christ, anyone, including the rich man, can enter into heaven. On the contrary, poor people aren't entitled to a special seat because of their deficiency. By confronting the rich man to sell every possession he owns, Jesus is bucking the prevailing view of the day that riches equate to happiness or blessedness. True joy comes not from things, but from a relationship with the Creator of all things.

Is he talking future service or present service? The immediacy of following Jesus as master today and not allowing money to consume a kingdom citizen shows how believers can be sidetracked with temporal things. One commentator summarized the point of this providential meeting: "Riches do not choke a person all at once. It is a gradual process. Like the weeds in Christ's parable, riches grow up gradually. Slowly, slowly, they strangle the budding of spiritual life within. Beware of that if you either have great possessions or are on your way to acquiring them. Above all, beware if you are saying, 'I need to provide for myself now. I'll think about spiritual things when I am older.'"[72]

The point of Jesus' parable is educational and discouraging at the same time. It's discouraging that only a small portion of believers will experience the abundant fruit-bearing life Jesus offers. I felt the effects of this truth after I shared the gospel on a plane flight with a professing atheist sitting next to me. The passenger said to me, "You're pretty narrow minded to believe that Jesus is the only way to God." I responded, "Jesus actually said himself that 'narrow is the way to life and difficult is the road and few people will find it'" (Matt. 7:13).

It's also educational to know that while some people fall away, some people digress, and some never grow as believers, Christ is not caught off guard. He foreknew and predicted what would transpire.

Kingdom Rule

After contrasting people living in the kingdom with those living outside of the kingdom, Jesus begins explaining how the kingdom advances with successive parables in Matthew: wheat and weeds, mustard seed, yeast, buried treasure, pearl of great price, and a fishing net. Let's reexamine familiar passages with this present-kingdom hermeneutic as a present reality instead of a future place to enter.

The kingdom is a process that accelerates mysteriously in spite of outsiders who are against it. The two opposing kingdoms, of God and of Satan, coexist at the same time. For example, Jesus compared the world to a garden where both kingdoms—the wheat and weeds—are intertwined. If you prematurely pull the weeds from the garden, you will damage the harvest.

> The kingdom of heaven may be compared to a man who sowed good seed in his field. But while people were sleeping, his enemy came, sowed weeds among the wheat, and left. When the plants sprouted and produced grain, then the weeds also appeared. The landowner's servants came to him and said, "Master, didn't you sow good seed in your field? Then where did the weeds come from?" "An enemy did this," he told them. "So, do you want us to go and pull them up?" the servants asked him. "No," he said. "When you pull up the weeds, you might also uproot the wheat with them. Let both grow together until the harvest. At harvest time I'll tell the reapers: 'Gather the weeds first and tie

them in bundles to burn them, but collect the wheat in my barn.'" (Matt. 13:24–30)

The kingdom is a grassroots movement that expands exponentially against all barriers or hindrances, much like a mustard seed tree grows in any environment. The kingdom is persistent and consistent.

> The kingdom of heaven is like a mustard seed that a man took and sowed in his field. It's the smallest of all the seeds, but when grown, it's taller than the garden plants and becomes a tree, so that the birds of the sky come and nest in its branches. (Matt. 13:31–32)

> The kingdom of heaven is like leaven that a woman took and mixed into fifty pounds of flour until all of it was leavened. (Matt. 13:33)

Seeking the kingdom should be the highest priority for a follower of Jesus. We must live with the same kingdom consciousness Jesus exemplified.

> The kingdom of heaven is like treasure, buried in a field, that a man found and reburied. Then in his joy he goes and sells everything he has and buys that field. (Matt. 13:44)

> The kingdom of heaven is like a merchant in search of fine pearls. When he found one priceless pearl, he went and sold everything he had and bought it. (Matt. 13:45–46)

The reality of the kingdom is that believers will one day be separated from unbelievers when Christ returns.

The kingdom of heaven is like a large net thrown into the sea. It collected every kind of fish, and when it was full, they dragged it ashore, sat down, and gathered the good fish into containers, but threw out the worthless ones. (Matt. 13:47–48)

Jones and Brown summarize Jesus' teachings on the kingdom by saying, "It is an expansive, rich and dynamic concept that cannot be boxed up or bottled up in nice little formulas, even if that frustrates those who want everything neatly spelled out in black and white."[73] By using many examples of different metaphors, Jesus demonstrates the multi-faceted nature of the kingdom.

Who Enters the Kingdom of God?

The disciples question Jesus on one of their short-term mission excursions about seat assignments in His kingdom: "So who is the greatest in the kingdom of heaven?" (Matt. 18:1). Much like many in churches today, each of them are thinking of a future event when they will sit on the twelve thrones judging Israel. Jesus corrects their misunderstanding by talking about a present entering today. "He called a child and had him stand among them. 'Truly I tell you,' he said, 'unless you turn and become like children, you will never enter the kingdom of heaven. Therefore, whoever humbles himself like this child—this one is the greatest in the kingdom of heaven. And whoever welcomes one child like this in my name welcomes me'" (Matt. 18:2–5). The context for entering the kingdom is now, not the future.

Similarly, the rule of God over people is evident in the short-term mission trip Jesus summoned the seventy to in Luke 10.

They were to leave behind money bags (what I jokingly refer to as the first fanny packs), suitcases, sandals, and swords. When a person greeted them in the name of peace, they should enter the house, teach about the kingdom, and remain with the family. For those who reject their message of the kingdom, the disciples were to announce the "kingdom of God has come near" before departing (Luke 10:11).

How could the kingdom come near? Kingdom citizens, the seventy disciples, were going before the king proclaiming His coming arrival. They weren't saying, "The kingdom is almost here" or "The king is about to arrive." Instead, they shouted, "The King is here! The King is here!" His arrival is marked by healing, deliverance, and salvation. When we go out to preach the gospel to a lost world, we, too, bring the kingdom message and kingdom power with us.

Two Men, Two Upbringings, and Two Outcomes

I've always been fascinated by Jesus' conversation with Zacchaeus, who was hanging from a sycamore tree in Jericho. If you were raised in church, you remember him as a "wee little man, and a wee little man was he." Locally, he wasn't known for his short stature but for his salvation experience. A tax collector was the most hated profession in all of Israel because they could impose any amount of money on the people at any time with the full authority of Rome behind them. Worse than that, these local tax collectors were Jewish-born individuals who became turn-coats on their own people. Jesus calls Zacchaeus out of the tree and says publicly, "It is necessary for me to stay at your house" (Luke 19:5). What is Jesus thinking? Doesn't He know this man's occupation? Every time you find "tax collector" in the Gospels it's attached to sinners or Gentiles (see Matt. 9:10, 11; 11:19; 18:17; 21:31, 32). Jewish men were discouraged from entering the home of tax collectors much less a revered Rabbi. Zacchaeus's response after Jesus welcomes him into His movement, along with his actions, displays kingdom conduct.

First, he exclaims, "Look, Lord!" (Luke 19:8 NIV). This title may appear bland on the surface, but Zacchaeus is making a kingdom statement. "Lord" is another title for master or king. We don't use it today in a democracy but in a monarchy, kings are referred to as Lord. Jesus is referred to as the "Lord of lords." When you acknowledge Jesus as Lord, you say, "You are in control. You are ruler and king of my life." Jesus exclaimed, "Why do you call me 'Lord, Lord,' and don't do the things I say?" (Luke 6:46). When a person used "Lord" in reference to a person, it signified they had relinquished control to that person.

The term *Lord* is used throughout Luke's Gospel to signify transformation. When Jesus encourages the early disciples to go on a fishing excursion after fishing all night, Peter questions Jesus' ability to catch fish: "*Master, . . .* we've worked hard all night long and caught nothing. But if you say so, I'll let down the nets" (Luke 5:5). He addresses Jesus as master or leader, which was customary to do. When he hauls in the largest catch to date, he bows in repentance and asks for forgiveness: "Go away from me, because I'm a sinful man, *Lord* (Luke 5:8). Jesus is no longer just a Rabbi or teacher but his Lord. When the leper approached Jesus asking for a healing, he said, "Lord, if you are willing, you can make me clean" (Matt. 8:2). The blind man uses the same word when he approaches Jesus for his sight, "Lord, let me recover my sight" (Mark 10:51 ESV).

Acknowledging Jesus as Lord is not just lip-service for Zacchaeus. The promised fruit of his life reveals the root of his heart: "Look, I'll give half of my possessions to the poor, Lord. And if I have extorted anything from anyone, I'll pay back four times as much" (Luke 19:8). He started the day far from Christ but ended it as a kingdom citizen.

Salvation is not a two-part process where we trust Him now for salvation and later for obedience. "We must dispense with the myth (all too common)," according to Sinclair Ferguson, "that we can have Christ as Saviour to begin the Christian life, and then at some later stage, make a full surrender to him as Lord."[74] Paul left us no wiggle room for waffling back and forth when he said, "If you confess with your mouth, 'Jesus is Lord,' and believe in your heart that God raised him from the dead, you will be saved" (Rom. 10:9). By confessing Jesus as Lord, we relinquish the throne of our own heart to King Jesus by acknowledging Him as Lord and Savior.

Another case study is Judas Iscariot, a man who started close to Jesus but ended far away. He even fooled the disciples up until the Last Supper as seen in the discussion around the table. Jesus disrupted the intimacy of the gathering with these words:

> "Truly, I say to you, one of you will betray me."
> And they were very sorrowful and began to say
> to him one after another, "Is it I, Lord?" He
> answered, "He who has dipped his hand in the
> dish with me will betray me. The Son of Man
> goes as it is written of him, but woe to that man
> by whom the Son of Man is betrayed! It would
> have been better for that man if he had not been
> born." (Matt. 26:20–24 ESV)

Peter inquires, "Is it I Lord?"

James asks, "Is it I Lord?"

John questions, "Is it I Lord?"

Matthew probes, "Is it I Lord?"

As the disciples's response resounded around the table, Judas is last to speak up. He states, "Is it I, Rabbi?" Jesus said to him, "You have said so" (Matt. 26:25 ESV). Judas witnessed every miracle, heard every message, and walked every mile. He gazed into the faces of the men and women healed from illnesses. He watched every deaf man hear, blind man see, and dead man be raised. He was sent out with the rest of the Twelve to cast out demons and heal the sick and with the seventy to proclaim the coming kingdom of God. He probably enjoyed Jesus' sermons and may have admired Jesus' compassion, but he had not relinquished control of his own heart. He was the king of his own kingdom. When push came to shove, he was unwilling to allow Jesus to reign supreme. At the conclusion of the ministry, he was still calling Jesus Rabbi, not Lord.

Judas may have fooled the disciples, but he didn't fool Jesus. Jesus disclosed Judas' identity early in their ministry when He said, "Didn't I choose you, the Twelve? Yet one of you is a devil" (John 6:70). Sadly, the disciples didn't pick up on it. What that shows us is that the wheat will grow among the weeds while the kingdom advances. Obviously, Judas was used as a pawn in the providential plan of God, but his allowance to stay among the disciples is interesting. Jesus didn't remove him immediately from the others for fear he would influence them, nor did Jesus pass on selecting him to follow Him. The kingdom of God still advanced in spite of his participation or lack thereof.

CHAPTER 8

God in Us: The Indwelling Presence of God

Without an understanding of the Jewish culture Jesus lived in, we can overlook subtle details of Jesus' life that have deep meaning. The feasts days on which Jesus died and rose are not coincidental. According to the apostle Paul, each one was given as a shadow of the coming Messiah (Col. 2:16–17). As the Lamb who takes away our sins, you would expect Jesus to die on the Day of Atonement or Yom Kippur. This annual feast was a day of national repentance from sin as the High Priest cleansed himself for six days leading up to the big day.

On the seventh day, the Day of Atonement, the high priest would rise and ceremonially cleanse himself again before making a sacrificial offering for himself and his household. Next, he would take two goats for two different purposes: one as a sin offering and the other as a *scapegoat*. He offered one goat as an offering to atone for the sin of the people, but the scapegoat was different. The priest would lay his hands on the goat's head and spiritually transpose the sins of the nation onto the animal. He then handed the goat off to a priest who was responsible for leading it into the desert. The reason God didn't choose this National Feast day for the death of His Son is because it communicated a different message. While Jesus' death atoned for the sins of those who would believe in Him, His death communicated another message.

Passover, at its conception, was about both freedom from bondage and submission to God's kingdom. The people were set free from one king to serve and worship another. Passover was a time when the nation remembered how God delivered their ancestors from Egypt in the past while praying for Him to set them free in the present. Freedom from Roman rule meant the advancement of God's kingdom now.

Passover screamed, "Liberation!"

Not liberation to serve oneself, but liberation to worship God.

Liberation to Worship God

The drama heightened from the first Passover to the zenith of all Passovers in Jesus' day. The death of an innocent animal started in Genesis when God made a sacrifice for Adam and Eve, and then made clothes out of the animal to cover their nakedness. We see another sacrifice with the offering of Isaac, a prototype of Christ, by his father Abraham. Before Abraham's hand descended upon his son, God provided a substitute for Isaac by offering a ram caught in the bushes (Genesis 22). One animal was replaced for one child. In Egypt, every household was required to kill an innocent lamb and apply the blood upon the doorposts of their homes as protection against the angel of death killing the unprotected firstborn sons (Exodus 12). A side note: God spares the firstborn sons of the nation in Exodus, but at

Calvary, He offers His one and only Son for our sins. One lamb was offered to cover the sins of one family.

On the Day of Atonement, the high priest offered one goat for the sins of the nation. When he placed his hand upon the head of the scapegoat, the sins of the nation were transferred onto the innocent animal. This was a vivid picture of one animal for the sins of the nation. When Christ was hanging on the cross, the sky turned strangely dark for three hours, signifying the sins of mankind being placed squarely upon the shoulders of Jesus, the innocent lamb of God. On Passover, God's work is done. One lamb, His Son, absorbed the sins of the world. He died the death that we deserved, and paid for the sins that we committed. What a Savior we have!

As kingdom citizens, we are free once and for all to serve King Jesus. Jesus taught this concept repeatedly through His ministry.

When Will You Return?

Up to this point, we have examined the importance of the tabernacle/Temple for the people, the embodiment of the Temple in the person and work of Jesus Christ, and the establishment of Jesus as King at the conclusion of His ministry, but you may be wondering, *What does this have to do with me? How am I able to live, move, and have purpose in the kingdom?*

The construction of a house for God to dwell among His people didn't end with the ascension of Jesus. In fact, the construction project was just beginning. Jesus alluded to this when He explained to His disciples, "Truly I tell you, the one who believes in me will also do the works that I do. And he will do even greater works than these, because I am going to the Father"

(John 14:12). I've heard some wrongly interpret this verse to mean the disciples would accomplish greater things in *significance* than Jesus. However, this is clearly not the case, for who can do anything superior to what God has done in Christ? What Jesus implied was that the *scope* of their ministries would be far-reaching. Jesus has in mind *quantity*, not *quality*. Because He is going to the Father, His ministry will multiply in the lives of the men and women who would come after Him as little temples housing the Holy Spirit (1 Cor. 6:19). The clearest picture is found at the beginning of Acts.

You may have wondered like I have about the topic of conversation during the forty-day period with Jesus from His resurrection to His ascension. Luke takes the guesswork out of our speculation by outlining the syllabus for the final course: "After he [Jesus] had suffered, he also presented himself alive to them by many convincing proofs, appearing to them over a period of forty days and *speaking about the kingdom of God*" (Acts 1:3).

Before Jesus wraps up the class, the disciples have one burning question to ask: "Lord, are your restoring the *kingdom to Israel* at this time?" (Acts 1:6). Let's be honest: if you were in their shoes, you would be wondering the same thing. But they are asking the wrong question. We can only imagine the dumbfounded expression Jesus has on His face. "Seriously? Are you guys still clueless about what the kingdom is like?" They expected fire from heaven upon their enemies, judgment for the wicked, punishment for the Romans, and on and on. Also, each was anticipating a seat at the apocalyptic table as well. Furthermore, their question is about the eschatological future kingdom and not the immediate kingdom as seen by Jesus' response, "It is not for you to know times or periods that the Father has set by his own authority" (Acts 1:7). This rebuttal can also be applied to our "end times" brothers and sisters today who occupy themselves with looking for every ominous harbinger as a sign of Christ's return.

Jesus redirects their attention to the kingdom at hand with the conjunction: "But you will receive power when the Holy Spirit has come on you, and you will be my witnesses in Jerusalem, in all Judea and Samaria, and to the end of the earth" (Acts 1:8). They didn't need to know when He was returning. What they needed to know was what to do until He returns. Surprisingly, Jesus encourages them to wait for ten days in prayer for the Spirit's power to fall. Don't go start your own ministries, don't set up that 501(c)(3) yet, and don't charge hell with a water pistol. Wait.

Waiting is tough. But the kingdom advances not just through our working but through our waiting.

- Noah endured mocking and humiliation for 120 years while he constructed the Ark.
- Abraham waited for twenty-five years before God came through on His covenantal promise.
- Joseph endured isolation in a pit and incarceration in a prison before realizing the promise God made to him thirteen years before.
- Moses wandered in the wilderness for four decades waiting to enter the land that was promised.
- Jesus waited thirty years before He began His earthly ministry.

Kingdom living requires patience, knowing God's timing is best because some virtues like trust, perseverance, and long-suffering are only learned through waiting. Remember, God works in our waiting. Jesus directed the disciples to wait so that His plan could come to fruition as ordered. The feast of Shavuot or Pentecost is inseparable from Passover. Similar to how our children count the days between Thanksgiving and Christmas, the Jewish people would count the "omers" or days from Passover to Pentecost. They waited fifty days to thank the Lord for providing the harvest. Both Passover and Pentecost were pilgrimage feasts that required all able Jews to return to Jerusalem to partake in the festival. Men and women from "all nations" would travel to Jerusalem on this day. Little did people know that this year they would get more than they bargained for. God would birth the church and unleash His kingdom at this time.

Spirit-Empowered Ministry

On the morning of Pentecost, when most were preparing for a day of worship, the devout pilgrims are in for a surprise as they are met by a small band of disciples acting rather odd.

> When the day of Pentecost had arrived, they were all together in one place. Suddenly a sound like that of a violent rushing wind came from heaven, and it filled the whole house where they were staying. They saw tongues like flames of fire that separated and rested on each one of them. Then they were all filled with the Holy Spirit and began to speak in different tongues, as the Spirit enabled them. (Acts 2:1–4)

I've always envisioned the fearful disciples huddled up in a cramped room waiting for the Spirit to fall upon them for the first time. However, a careful reading of the Gospels and Acts reveals otherwise. The final lines of Luke's Gospel, which dovetails into Acts, reads: "After worshiping him, they returned to Jerusalem with great joy. And they were continually *in the temple* praising God" (Luke 24:52–53). This doesn't sound like petrified men fearing for their lives. The disciples had no reason to be afraid, for they had already been filled with the Holy Spirit in when Jesus breathed His Spirit into them: "And when he had said this, he breathed on them and said to them, 'Receive the Holy Spirit. If you forgive the sins of any, they are forgiven them; if you withhold forgiveness from any, it is withheld'" (John 20:22–23 ESV). Acts 2, then, is another filling of the Holy Spirit. Paul suggested this would happen repeatedly throughout one's life: "be filled [continuously] with the Spirit" (Eph. 5:18 NIV). We are indwelt once but filled repeatedly with God's Spirit as we submit to His authority.

Also, the disciples were probably not in a house like we imagine today, for what house in first-century Israel could hold 120 disciples, much less one today? They were probably gathered in the Temple courts worshiping God. The "house of God" is a common phrase used to describe the Temple, and the rushing wind accompanied with tongues of fire most likely appeared in front of thousands of worshipers in the Temple complex.[75] God used "house" to describe His "Temple" when He declared to David: "When your time comes to be with your fathers, I will raise up after you your descendant, who is one of your own sons, and I will establish his *kingdom*. He is the one who will build a *house* for me, and I will establish his throne forever" (1 Chron. 17:11–12). The word *house* in Hebrew can be translated as dwelling place, family, lineage, or temple.[76]

God envisioned a day when His spirit would indwell a body of people permanently. "King David," asserts Tverberg, "had wanted to build God a 'house,' a temple, but God instead declared that He would build David a 'house' in terms of a royal family lineage. At Pentecost, the Spirit indwelt the hearts of the believers. The people of the early church would have recalled other scenes of God's Spirit entering His Temple, as it did in Solomon's day (2 Chron. 7:1–3)."[77]

It is no coincidence that Exodus ends with God dedicating the tabernacle with "fire inside the cloud by night, visible to the entire house of Israel throughout all the stages of their journey" (Exod. 40:38). After God took up residence in the tabernacle, He presided there. Again, when Solomon dedicated the Temple building, God consumed it with fire to signify His presence. When God birthed the church, believers were filled with tongues of fire as the Spirit inhabited the new Temple. Tverberg continues, "Now we can see a progression of God's plan to have intimacy with humankind, even though we forfeited our relationship with Him through sin. When God first commanded Israel to build a tabernacle the purpose was not just so He could dwell in it but could dwell *among them* (Exod. 29:45). Then He commissioned Solomon to build the Temple and filled it with His presence. Finally, through the atoning work of Christ, God came to indwell our hearts as His *bayit*, His house [temple], and achieve His greatest goal of living intimately with His people."[78] In AD 30, Pentecost marked the filling of the Temple with God's glory; only this time, the dwelling place is not a building but born-again believers.

Re-Righting the Curse of Babel

After Peter preaches the gospel to the crowd in Acts 2, three thousand people responded to His message to trust Christ as Lord and Savior. A motley crew, mustard seed movement expands from 120 in Acts 1 to 3,120 in one day. There are now three thousand born-again infants in Christ to care for. What did the disciples do?

After baptism, did the disciples say to the new converts:

> "We're glad you made a decision. Pull yourself up by your own sandals and come to service next week"?

> Did they report numbers to the Jerusalem Christian Convention?

> Did they give them flyers to invite people to a week-long crusade to hear the apostles give evangelistic messages?

They did none of the above. I believe they emulated what Jesus modeled before them. The disciples discipled the new converts in how to live in the kingdom of heaven today.

I asked myself the question: Why not four hundred or four thousand? Why not 3,001 or 3,050? The Bible makes it clear that three thousand came to faith in Christ that day. Numbers in the Bible are significant. Take for instance, the number *seven* which signifies completion or wholeness as seen in the seventh day of the week or sabbath. Seven is a number that cannot be improved upon. The root word of the number *seven* in Hebrew (*sheba'*) can be translated as "satisfied" or "full." We find this number throughout the Hebrew Bible: the sabbatical year is the seventh year, the year of Jubilee was after seven times seven years or forty-nine. Three of Israel's feasts take place in the seventh month: the Feast of Trumpets, the Day of Atonement, and the Feast of Tabernacles. God instituted seven feasts for Israel to observe. The number of weeks from Passover to Pentecost is seven. When God instructed Joshua to destroy Jericho with music, He emphasized the number seven: enlist seven priests, and seven trumpeters, for seven days of marching, divided into seven Circuits around the city, and expect God to move on the seventh day (Joshua 4). God's sovereign fingerprints were all over that plan. The same could be said about the numbers *three* and *forty*. One number that may be unfamiliar is the number three thousand.

Since Jesus fulfilled the Old Testament Scriptures with His life (Matt. 5:17), He, therefore, fulfilled every one of the seven feasts God gave Moses on the mountain of Sinai. Jesus died on Passover, was buried on the day of the Feast of Unleavened Bread, was raised on the celebration of First Fruits, and descended from heaven in the power of the Holy Spirit on Pentecost. His life, death, and resurrection paralleled the festivals of Israel. One feast is connected with the number *three thousand*. Can you name it? The first Pentecost.

After leading the Israelites out of Egypt on the first Passover, Moses traveled for forty-seven days before resting at the base of Mount Sinai for an encounter with the living God on the following day. After meeting God on day forty-eight, Moses was given instructions: "Go to the people and consecrate them *today* and *tomorrow*. They must wash their clothes and be prepared by the *third* day, for on the *third* day the LORD will come down on Mount Sinai in the sight of all the people" (Exod. 19:10–11). Moses ascended the mountain on the third day, which was day fifty, to receive the law—the exact day Pentecost would fall from that moment on.

Jubilation over God's Word given to the people would have to wait. When Moses began his descent down the mountain, he noticed the Israelites worshiping a golden calf they had forged out of their jewelry. He was exceedingly angry and delivered a scathing word from God: "This is what the Lord, the God of Israel, says, 'Every man fasten his sword to his side; go back and forth through the camp from entrance to entrance, and each of you kill his brother, his friend, and his neighbor.'" The text then tells us that "about *three thousand* men fell dead that day among the people" (Exod. 32:27–28).

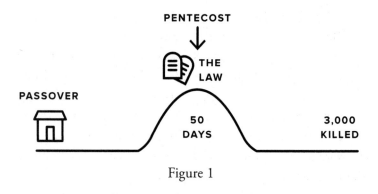

Figure 1

How does this connect to Acts 2? We notice a connection between the events of the Exodus and the death and ascension of Christ. On Passover, Jesus was crucified on a mountain while the sacrificial lambs were being slaughter for the feast. He devoted forty days in His resurrected body to "speaking about the kingdom of God" (Acts 1:3) before ascending to heaven. The disciples waited ten more days until day fifty for God to pour out His Spirit on Pentecost. After Peter preached his emboldened sermon in Acts 2, something remarkable happened: "So those who accepted his message were baptized, and that day about three thousand people were added to them" (Acts 2:41).

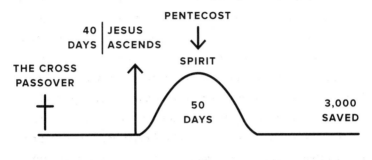

Figure 2

While the original Passover spared the nation of Israel, it could not transform their hardened hearts, so the people fell back into idolatry. Sadly, the giving of God's commandments on Sinai was followed by disobedience and death. But at Pentecost, God's law was written, not on stone tablets, but on the hearts of men and women by His Spirit. The reversal of the effects of death can be seen in the number of people who got saved. Just as God gave His word on the mountain of Sinai, Peter preached the Word on Mount Jerusalem.

Even today, Jewish communities reenact a wedding ceremony on Pentecost by reading the Ten Commandments and chanting, "We will do and hear."[79] Here is a ketubah, a wedding contract, written by a sixteenth-century poet Israel Najara, that was read on Pentecost every year:

> The Invisible One came forth from Sinai
> . . . in the year 2448 since the creation. The
> Bridegroom, Ruler of rulers said unto the pious,
> lovely and virtuous bride, the people of Israel,

who won His favor, who is beautiful as the moon, radiant as the sun, awesome as bannered hosts: "Be thou My mate according to the law of Moses and Israel, and I will honor, support, and maintain thee and be thy shelter and refuge in everlasting mercy.

This bride, Israel, consented and became His Spouse. Thus an eternal covenant, binding them forever, was established between them. The Bridegroom then agreed to add to the above all future expositions of Scripture. The dowry that this bride brought form the house of her father consists of an understanding heart that understands, ears that hearken, and eyes that see. All these conditions are valid and established forever and ever.

I invoke heaven and earth as reliable witnesses. May the Bridegroom rejoice with the bride whom He has taken as His lot and may the bride rejoice with the Husband of her youth while uttering words of praise.[80]

When fire-like tongues spoke with sounds of rushing wind on Mount Jerusalem at Pentecost, the crowd knew immediately what was happening. The story they've recited and reenacted yearly is being recreated before their very eyes. (Imagine if you had a front row seat that day to witness it.) God is instituting a New Covenant, similar to His former covenant, with His people. Only this time, the law will not be written on stone tablets, but on human hearts.

As a result of Jesus fulfilling the believers with the indwelling power of the Holy Spirit as the new Temple, it's no wonder most of the controversies in the book of Acts pertain to temples. Stephen is tried for crimes against the Temple (Acts 6–7). Paul engages in a confrontation with the local temple cult in Acts 14, with the temples in Athens and Ephesus in Acts 17 and 19, and over the Temple in Jerusalem on multiple occasions in Acts 21:28–29; 24:6; 25:8.[81] In the Old Testament, God first dwelt among His people in the tabernacle, and then in the Temple. But beginning in the New Testament, God builds believers themselves—the church—into His dwelling place.[82] *In the Old Testament, God built a Temple for His people, but in the New Testament, God formed a people to be His Temple.*

SECTION 3

Kingdom Conduct

CHAPTER 9

Kingdom-Minded Ministry

K ingdom living aligns with the rule and standard of King Jesus as opposed to the desires of oneself. When we submit to "walk by the Spirit and not by the flesh," as Paul suggest in Galatians 5, God's kingdom agenda advances in our lives. John Stackhouse rightly asserts, "We see the marks of the kingdom of God, then, wherever light penetrates darkness, wherever good makes its way against evil or inertia, wherever beauty emerges amid ugliness and vapidity, and wherever truth sounds out against error or falsity."[83] The book of Acts is a collection of encounters where the early believers proclaimed Jesus as King and called for others to surrender to Him.

The kingdom agenda is seen in passages such as:

> Acts 8:12: "But when they believed Philip, as he proclaimed the good news about the *kingdom of God* and the name of Jesus Christ, both men and women were baptized.

> Acts 19:8: "Paul entered the synagogue and spoke boldly over a period of three months,

arguing and persuading them about the *kingdom of God.*

Acts 20:25: "And now I know that none of you, among whom I went about *preaching the kingdom,* will ever see me again."

Acts 28:23–24: "After arranging a day with him, many came to him at his lodging. From dawn to dusk he expounded and testified about the *kingdom of God.* He tried to persuade them about Jesus from both the Law of Moses and the Prophets. Some were persuaded by what he said, but others did not believe."

Acts 28:30–31: "Paul stayed two whole years in his own rented house. And he welcomed all who visited him, proclaiming the *kingdom of God* and teaching about the Lord Jesus Christ with all boldness and without hindrance."

Romans 14:17: "The *kingdom of God* is not eating and drinking, but righteousness, peace, and joy in the Holy Spirit.

1 Corinthians 4:20: "For the *kingdom of God* is not a matter of talk but of power.

1 Corinthians 15:50: "What I am saying, brothers and sisters, is this: Flesh and blood cannot inherit the *kingdom of God,* nor can corruption cannot inherit incorruption."

Colossians 1:13: "He has rescued us from the domain of darkness and transferred us into the *kingdom* of the Son he loves." Notice the past-tense promise here. God has transferred us (past) into the kingdom of Christ (present) at salvation.

Hebrews 12:28–29: "Therefore, since we are receiving a *kingdom* that cannot be shaken, let us be thankful. By it, we may serve God acceptably, with reverence and awe, for our God is a consuming fire.

What does this look like in our lives today? McNeal is helpful in highlighting three aspects of God's kingdom: "The way of the kingdom is a *spirit*, an *attitude*, and a *life* that honor God and allow us to serve as collaborators with him in helping others experience the life he intends for them."[84]

Moreover, when Paul states in Philippians "our citizenship is in heaven" (Phil. 3:20), he doesn't envision believers writing off this world in hopes of leaving for heaven. Christians, at the moment of salvation become citizens of heaven while still holding passports on Earth. This is precisely why Peter urges Christians "as strangers and exiles to abstain from sinful desires that wage war against the soul" (1 Pet. 2:11). *Our identity influences our activity.* A passport is required to travel out of the country you have citizenship in. The stamp on your passport upon entering a foreign county is a reminder that you don't live there. As a visitor, you're just passing through. Similarly, it should be clear thus that after our born-again experience, we are citizens of another kingdom—a heavenly one.

Citizenship is a way of describing our belonging to a specific group. Without understanding the context in which Paul is writing, these words lose the impact they once had. Many of the inhabitants of Philippi were Roman citizens with intense pride in being a citizen of Rome (similar to American patriotism). Even though they were citizens of Rome, their allegiance was to Christ and His kingdom. The demands of God's kingdom superseded the expectations of Roman leaders such as Nero or Domitian.

An unknown Christian writer of the second century developed the apostle's thought in a memorable passage. In the Epistle to Diognetus, he describes the true Christian character and conduct as follows:

> Christians sever themselves from others, neither in dwelling nor language. . . . They inhabit their own fatherland but they do so as foreigners. They do whatever is their duty as citizens, and yet suffer all things as aliens. . . . They live in the flesh, but not according to the flesh. They dwell on earth, but they live in heaven. They obey the existing laws, but by their conduct they exalt themselves above the laws. They are poor, and yet make many rich. They dwell in the world, and yet are not of it. They are seen as dwellers in the world, but their true life is unseen. They are hated of the world, although they are benefiting it by contending with its evil. . . . Such is the noble office assigned by God to His people, and they dare not decline it.[85]

A Community of Royal Priests

As a result of the death, burial, and resurrection of Jesus, kingdom citizens are expected to bear His image to a lost world. We accomplish this through living as "a chosen race, a royal priesthood, a holy nation, a people for his possession, so that you may proclaim the praises of the one who called you out of darkness into his marvelous light" (1 Pet. 2:9).[86] Why does God insert the word "royal," indicating Kingship, before "priesthood"? The same reference is found in Revelation. In Revelation 1:5–6, we are told that God "loves us and has set us free from our sins by his blood, and made us a kingdom, priests to his God and Father— to him be glory and dominion forever and ever. Amen."

Peter's language is reminiscent of Exodus 19 where God says virtually the same thing about the nation of Israel after rescuing them from Egypt: "You have seen what I did to the Egyptians and how I carried you on eagles' wings and brought you to myself. Now if you will carefully listen to me and keep my covenant, you will be my own possession out of all the peoples, although the whole earth is mine, and you *will be my kingdom of priests* and my holy nation" (Exod. 19:4–6). God outlines the kind of relationship He desires before he ever gives them the commandments.

The job of a priest in God's economy was twofold: to worship God (priestly duties) and be a witness for God (royal duties).[87] In a sense, his job was to bring people to God. However, with great privilege came great responsibility. Certain stipulations were put on their lives. For example, priests couldn't fight in battles (Num. 1:44–50), nor could they own land (Deut. 18:1–2).

These men were visible reflections of the invisible God to the people around them while mediating a relationship between God and man. By applying this identity to New Testament believers, Peter was commissioning us as ambassadors to mediate God in Christ to the world. The chief requirement for living as a priest was being "set apart" or "sanctified" from sin and the world. Holiness was essential for service to God. The modifier "royal" implies living in a kingdom over which Christ rules as king. Commentator Karen Jobes wrote, "The kingdom of God is composed of believers who must think of themselves as holy with respect to the world, set apart for purity and a purpose demanded by God. This is the priesthood that serves the King of the universe."[88] They lived differently than the world to make a difference in the world. What's changed after Jesus inaugurated the kingdom with His coming was that "all people are priests, and all the priests are the people" in the kingdom of heaven today.[89]

God communicated to Pharaoh through Moses the reason for setting His people free: "Let my people go, so that they may worship me" (Exod. 9:1). The book of Exodus culminates with worship of God through the construction of the tabernacle, not with what we may expect, the giving of the law (Exodus 20). Our present involvement in the world as priests is a foreshadowing of our future, active involvement in Christ's work tomorrow. "The new people of God are not *in* a Temple, attending a service led by priests, they *are* the temple and they *are* its priests, themselves conducting the service."[90] The present reality of our task is seen in Revelation 5 as the people sang, "You are worthy to take the scroll and to open its seals, because you were slaughtered, and you purchased people for God by your blood from every tribe and language and people and nation. You *made them* a kingdom and priests to our God, and they will reign on the earth" (Rev. 5:9–10).

The promise of Exodus 19, "you will be my kingdom of priests," is realized in Revelation 5, "you made them a kingdom of priests," as a completed action.[91] If we couple this promise/ fulfillment aspect with Peter's declaration that "we are a royal priesthood," each of us will understand our current role in the unfolding plan of God in the present world.

How is this accomplished? Jesus gave us a clue before departing. When the disciples asked about Jesus restoring the kingdom in Acts 1, He redirects their attention to their individual kingdom assignments: "You will receive power when the Holy Spirit has come on you, and you will be my *witnesses* in Jerusalem, in all Judea and Samaria, and to the end of the earth" (Acts 1:8).

Image Bearers

"Witness" is the Greek word *martureo* where we get the English word *martyr*. A witness is someone who reflects the image of something or someone. Similar to billboards that line the shoulders of interstate highways project a message to watchful drivers. A mirror would be another example of a witness. In the same way a mirror reflects an image off the glass, believers are to reflect the king to those around them.

Other usages of witness are found in Acts 2:32, "God has raised this Jesus; we are all *witnesses* of the fact" and Acts 3:15, "You killed the source of life, whom God raised from the dead; we are *witnesses* of this." Believers don't choose if they are a witness or not, they simply are. We are either good ones or poor ones.

God's glory, then, is reflected by us. If we journey back to the beginning of creation, we notice that God formed man in order to bear His image: "So God created man in his own image; he created him in the image of God; he created them male and female" (Gen. 1:27). The Jewish Sages note the reputation of the word *image* as significant. God doesn't want us to miss its significance. Man was created to reflect the image of the invisible God to the world, similar to the way Jesus did while on Earth: "He is the image of the invisible God, the firstborn over all creation" (Col. 1:15).

The enemy of image-bearing is idolatry. Jesus teaches this lesson while answering a trick question about paying taxes to Caesar. Every adult male in Judea was forced to pay taxes (called a poll tax or head tax) directly to the Imperial treasury. The sum of the tax was an entire day's wage. The Denarius coin that was to be given bore the "image" of the emperor. The silver coin was stamped with the image of Tiberius Caesar. Underneath his face was the abbreviated Latin inscription *Tiberius Caesar Divi Augusti Filius Augustus* ("Tiberius Caesar Augustus, Son of the Divine Augustus").[92] The opposite side bore an image of Tiberius's mother Livia and had the inscription, *Pontif Maxim* ("High Priest"), both claims were titles reserved for the Messiah. Jews were forbidden from carrying this coin with them, for God prohibited idolatry.[93]

"Tiberius Caesar Augustus, Son of the Divine Augustus"

What appeared to be an honest question is an act of hypocrisy: "Tell us, then, what you think. Is it lawful to pay taxes to Caesar, or not" (Matt. 22:17 ESV). Jesus' response exposed the motivation of their hearts: "Perceiving their malicious intent, Jesus said, "Why are you testing me, hypocrites?" (Matt. 22:18). It's a no-win situation for Jesus. On the one hand, if He answers no, they will charge Him with rebelling against Rome; on the other hand, if He answers yes, He will be siding with Rome and alienating the nation of Israel.

When Jesus asked for a coin, He indicted His attackers by proving their utter disregard for God's commandments. They claimed to be followers outwardly but cut theological corners inwardly. Jewish people should have never possessed this coin for it was only used for paying tax, unlike the Jewish shekel which was used for everyday business. Their question was about commerce, but Jesus' concern is about their commitment to God.

In Whose Image

Jesus initiated the discussion, "'Whose image and inscription is this?' he asked them. 'Caesar's,' they said to him. Then he said to them, 'Give, then, to Caesar the things that are Caesar's, and to God the things that are God's.' When they heard this, they were amazed. So they left him and went away" (Matt. 22:20–22).

Tiberius, the Caesar in Jesus' day, minted coins with his image on them, affirming his belief of being the highest religious figure in the Empire. This assertion was offensive to the Jewish people because it is a violation of the Second Commandment: "You shall not make graven images of God." Warren Wiersbe unpacks Jesus' response: "Caesar's image is on his coins, so they must be minted by his authority. The fact that you possess these coins and use them, indicates that you think they are worth something. Therefore, you are already accepting Caesar's authority or you would not use his money. But you are created in the image of God, and therefore must live under God's authority as well."[94]

By contrasting what is owed to Caesar and what is owed to God, Jesus rejected Caesar's claim of being the divine high priest and stresses the importance of devotion reserved only for God. The image-bearing concept was not a new concept for them, for God instituted the idea back in the garden of Eden with the creation of mankind.

Remember what Genesis proposed: "God created man in his own *image*; he created him in the *image* of God; he created them male and female (Gen. 1:27). The self-prescribed leaders of Israel struggled with divided loyalties, something Jesus warned against repeatedly throughout His ministry as a hindrance to living in the kingdom. He told His disciples on one occasion, "If anyone comes to me and does not hate his own father and mother, wife and children, brothers and sisters—yes, and even his own life—he cannot be my disciple. Whoever does not bear his own cross and come after me cannot be my disciple" (Luke 14:26–27).[95] The word *hate* is translated "love less" in this passage. Jesus expects allegiance to him above every person or possession in our life.

Jesus requested a coin. The leaders indict themselves by producing the coin. No Jew should have carried that coin; certainly not the religious leaders of the day. Jesus asked, "Whose image is on the coin?" Give that to Caesar then. Here's what Jesus implies: "These coins belong to Caesar because his image is stamped on them, so give him what's his. But, what image is stamped upon you?" As image-bearers of God, you are aliens and foreigners on Earth because your citizenship is in the kingdom of heaven. Since humanity bears God's image, you belong to Him! Jesus is not concerned with whether we pay taxes or not (although it would have been nice for Him to free us from paying Uncle Sam); He is concerned here with their divided loyalties. Like the coin in their hand, the people are waffling between two sides. They are straddling the fence in their devotion, therefore, giving themselves over to idolatry.

Idolatry is not just carved images on a shelf or in a church for people to pray and adore. It covers what consumes your hearts affection and mind attention. We engage in idolatry in four ways:

- Worshiping something or someone other than God (Deut. 8:17; Dan. 4:30; 5:22–23).
- Seeking security in something or someone other than God (Jer. 2:13, 18; 1 Tim. 6:17)
- Desiring something or someone other than God (Matt. 6:24; Eph. 5:5).
- Setting our affections elsewhere by being unwilling to part with someone or something for God.

The revivalist Leonard Ravenhill often said, "Anything you love more than Jesus Christ is an idol."[96] What are the idols in your life? Is it your business? Is it your reputation? Is it your worldly success? Is it self-centeredness? Do you covet things? Is it the pursuit of power or prestige? Is it a relationship or the desire to have one? As pastors, deacons, or elders, it's easy to fall in love with the ministry of Jesus and out of love with Jesus who gave them the ministry in the first place.

The image of God has been disfigured since the Fall as a result of Adam's sin. God restored our relationship with Him through the finished work of Christ on the cross. By repenting of our sins, we give Jesus absolute authority over our lives. Will you give to Caesar what is Caesar's (we could insert America's), and give to God what is God's? You may be asking, "How does one do this? Obedience. "We can only accomplish our mission," believes Beale, "as we recognize our identity as icons of God."[97] Therefore, as kingdom citizens who bear the image of our King, we should never doubt our self-worth. We are God's prized possessions because we bear His image. He sends us out as witnesses of this truth to a lost world seeking identity and worth in things other than Him.

Obeying the King

Every person resides in a present kingdom, most with self-appointed kings. As John Calvin remarked, "Everyone flatters himself and carries a kingdom in his breast."[98] Although, God's rule is exclaimed in Exodus, man's rule is explained in Genesis 1. In his book *The Divine Conspiracy*, Dallas Willard writes,

> The human job description (the "creation covenant," we might call it) found in chapter 1 of Genesis indicates that God assigned to us collectively the rule over all living things on Earth, animal and plant. We are responsible before God for life on the Earth (vv. 28–30). However unlikely it may seem from our current viewpoint, God equipped us for this task by framing our nature to function in a conscious, personal relationship of interactive responsibility with him. We are meant to exercise our "rule" only in union with God, as he acts with us.[99]

As a result of our surrendering to Him, our dominion or rule expands. When God can trust us with small tasks, He will entrust us with greater things. Kingdom economics is explained in the parable of the talents when Jesus declares, "Well done," to the faithful servant. He goes on, "You were faithful over a few things; I will put you in charge of many things. Share your master's joy'" (Matt. 25:23). Obedience is the distinctive marker to kingdom living, for Jesus said, "Those who love me obey me" (John 14:23).

Often, I hear Christians erroneously saying that the Old Testament doesn't apply to them anymore. Notice how Jesus addressed those very thoughts: "Don't think that I came to abolish the Law or the Prophets. I did not come to abolish but to fulfill. For truly I tell you, until heaven and earth pass away, not the smallest letter or one stroke of a letter will pass away from the law until all things are accomplished" (Matt. 5:17–18).

Jesus sums up the Hebrew Bible, our Old Testament, with the phrase "the Law or the Prophets." He didn't come to *abolish* but to *fulfill*. *Abolish* can be translated as destroy, demolish, or misinterpret. *Fulfill* means to establish or complete something by design. A simple translation would be to "fill full" of something.

When I was younger, I wanted to be an artist, among the other hobbies I was pursuing—guitar player, magician, basketball athlete, comic book and coin collector, DJ, and video gamer—so my parents enrolled me in art lessons (as a kid my nickname was Hobby Robby). Before paint could be applied to the canvas, the image had to be first pencil sketched as a foreshadowing of the finished product. After completing the design, paint could fill in the lines. Likewise, the Old Testament commands are the pencil sketch drawing of the coming Messiah. They were incomplete until Jesus, so to speak, painted between the lines with His life. He completed the portrait.[100]

Jesus fulfilled the Law or Torah in three ways: prophecy, life, and death. The Old Testament contains more than three hundred messianic prophecies about the Christ. Jesus fulfilled all of them. We could say the Abrahamic covenant portrayed the promise of the Messiah, the Mosaic covenant (law) gave a picture of the Messiah, and the New Covenant introduced us to the person who is the Messiah.

Jesus' life exemplified one of devotion to God and His commandments. Jesus never broke the written law, as wrongfully accused by the religious leaders of His day; He disregarded the oral law of the Pharisees which lost the heart and intent of God. John Philips writes,

> The Jews counted 613 separate edicts in the Mosaic law and there never was a single moment when the Lord Jesus did not absolutely fulfill in every detail every commandment. As a baby and as a boy, as a teenager and in the prime of life, at home, at school, at work, at play, as a son and as a brother, as a neighbor and as a friend, as a village carpenter, as an itinerant preacher, in secret and in public, when surrounded by family and friends and when confronted by formidable foes—at all times, in all places, in all ways, He kept the law of God. He kept it in letter and in spirit. He kept the law in its injunctions and in its intentions. He kept it because it was His nature to keep it. He would never dream of not keeping it. It was His Father's will and Jesus always did those things that please the Father.[101]

Jesus exemplified for His disciples what was expected from His father.

Finally, Jesus fulfilled the Torah in His death. As the second Adam, Jesus stood in our place, satisfying the righteous demands of the law by accomplishing what Adam was incapable of doing.

Where Adam failed, Jesus was faithful. Kent Hughes describes the effects of the law on the life of the people:

> In his experiments Ivan Pavlov would ring a bell whenever he fed his dogs. Eventually the dogs would salivate whenever they heard the bell. They knew the bell meant food for them. The sacrifices of the Old Testament prepared the people by instilling in them the conditioned reflex that sacrifice meant death. And the Old Testament sacrifices prepared them for the Lord Jesus' death when He came to die for our sins. Jesus fulfilled what the sacrificial system had pointed to.[102]

If we apply Western logic to an Eastern word, the meaning can get lost in the translation.[103] *Fulfill* should not be translated in a linear fashion signifying completion, as it does in our culture. In this respect, once the promise, order, or event is fulfilled, it is no longer useful for anything.

We witness this reality every August as Old Navy mails out catalogs with their 30 percent off Back to School sale. (I've since realized Old Navy has a year round 30 percent off sale.) Even though I'm not in school, I decided to get online and order some new jeans. The process is simple: you select a pair of jeans, choose your size, click the order button, type in your credit card number, and hit "submit." At that moment, you enter into a contract. The payment of your money triggers the company to send your product. Next, the order is emailed to a fulfillment warehouse before the jeans are packaged and mailed out. When the jeans arrive, do I have any more use for the catalog? Would I ever go back and view the pictures of the purchased jeans online again?

No. After receiving the product, the order was complete and the promise was fulfilled.

If we interpret Jesus' words in this manner, we miss His point. By fulfilling the Old Testament, He didn't diminish, disband, or disestablish the Torah. He didn't blur the lines; He painted within them with His life. He moved the Old Testament from black and white to high definition color. It makes sense that He came to interpret it correctly.

I Love the Torah

My favorite TV show is *Live PD* on A&E. Before that it used to be *Cops*. No exaggeration, I've probably seen every *Cops* episode. From Coco the Clown to the high-speed chases that end up with canine pursuits, one thing is constant: no one is excited when the law shows up. The Jewish people, however, had a different view than we do. In fact, an entire psalm is devoted to the benefits and attributes of God's law in the Old Testament. In the middle of the passage, the psalmist cites, "How I love your instruction! It is my meditation all day long" (Ps. 119:97). This was the pervading view of God's Torah or instruction for the Old Testament saints and New Covenant believers in Christ.

> Romans 3:31: "Do we then nullify the law through faith? Absolutely not! On the contrary, we uphold the law."

> Romans 7:12: "So then, the law is holy, and the commandment is holy and just and good."

> Romans 7:14: "For we know that the law is spiritual, but I am of the flesh, sold as a slave to sin."

Romans 8:4: "In order that the law's requirement would be fulfilled in us who do not walk not according to the flesh but according to the Spirit."

1 Corinthians 7:19: "Circumcision does not matter and uncircumcision does not matter. Keeping the commandments of God is what matters."

1 Corinthians 10:23: "'Everything is permissible,' but not everything is beneficial. 'Everything is permissible,' but not everything builds up.'"

Galatians 5:1: "For freedom, Christ set us free. Stand firm then and don't submit again to a yoke of slavery."

How do you view the law? Are God's commandments restrictions of your happiness or expression of His love for you? The Jewish culture viewed the law differently than we do today. The law, for most, emits feelings of anxiety as we imagine getting pulled over for doing something we shouldn't. Nobody jumped out of bed this morning and thought, "I can't wait to obey the laws of my state today" or "I'm looking forward to driving 55 mph on the interstate to work tomorrow." The Jewish people, on the other hand, viewed God's commandments differently.

1. The Torah, as they referred to the Law, was direction, instruction, aim, or guidance for life.

Your word is a lamp to my feet and a light to my path. (Ps. 119:105 ESV)

Success in God's economy was determined by how well one followed His word. Before Joshua entered the Promised Land, God instructed the people, "This book of instruction [Torah] must not depart from your mouth; you are to meditate on it day and night so that you may carefully observe everything written in it. For then you will prosper and succeed in whatever you do" (Josh. 1:8). In a similar fashion, Psalm 1 outlines a pleasing life to God: "How happy is the one who does not walk in the advice of the wicked or stand in the pathway with sinners or sit in the company of mockers! Instead, his delight is in the LORD's instruction [Torah], and he meditates on it day and night" (Ps. 1:1–2).

2. The Torah should be treasured.

> You remove all the wicked on earth as if they were dross from metal; therefore, I *love* your decrees. (Ps. 119:119)

One hundred seventy-six verses of Psalm 119 are devoted to extolling the wonders of God's Word. God's Word was how man and woman fostered a relationship with their Creator.

3. The Torah was given through God's Spirit.

God wrote the law with His own finger (Deut. 9:10; Luke 11:20). We know God doesn't have fingers, so Moses uses what's called an anthropomorphism—ascribing a human characteristic to the behavior of God to demonstrate how His Spirit carved out the commandments on the tablets. "On the day of the assembly the LORD gave me the two stone tablets, inscribed by God's finger" (Deut. 9:10).

4. The Torah was viewed as a gift of grace.

We realize this with the giving of the Law after God saved the people from Egypt. Our understanding of grace being without strings attached and expecting nothing in return is a modern notion. According to John Barclay in his exhaustive book, *Paul and the Gift*, Paul appeals to the popular opinions of the day and issues a clarion call for reversing our understanding of grace. Looking at it one-sided has hindered this robust concept in the ancient world. By investigating biblical and extra-biblical sources, and studies in culture and context of the first century, Barclay suggests that grace as a "pure gift"—expecting nothing in return for a gift—is unfounded in the world of Jesus and Paul.[104] (For a comprehensive look at this concept see: John Barclay, *Paul and the Gift*.)

Although the gift may have been given freely, it was understood that the recipient would reciprocate the act of kindness. There were three aspects to a gift in that culture: "the obligation to give, the obligation to receive, and the obligation to return."[105] Returning the favor for receiving something was the unwritten rule of the biblical world. No one ever received a "no strings attached" gift. We are able to view passages on salvation in the New Testament such as Ephesians 2:8–9; Romans 3:23–24; and Titus 2:11 differently. An example of reciprocity in regards to grace is clearly seen in 1 Peter 4:10, "Just as each one has received a *gift*, use it to serve others, as good stewards of the varied *grace* of God."

5. Jesus embodied the Torah.

If the Torah were unimportant, why did Jesus spend three years of His life fulfilling it? He could have easily walked into the Temple as a teenager proclaiming that He was the Messiah. The leaders would have labeled Him a heretic; He would have died, resurrected, and ascended to heaven just as He did years later. None of this happened because *Jesus' life was just as important as Jesus' death*. He promised, "Truly I tell you, until heaven and earth pass away, not the smallest letter or one stroke of a letter will pass away from the law until all things are accomplished" (Matt. 5:17–18). This approach to the law is starkly different than what many have been taught for years.

The Messiah's Law

Are you saying that I need to keep the law today?

Because of Christ, New Covenant believers are "not under law but under grace" (Rom. 6:14) as Paul made clear in Romans; however, we are enrolled into a new agreement. Paul made this clear to the church at Corinth: "To those who are without the law, like one without the law—though I am not without God's law but under the *law* of Christ—to win those without the law" (1 Cor. 9:21). Again, we see this in Romans 8:1–2, "Therefore, there is now no condemnation for those in Christ Jesus,' because the *law* of the Spirit of life in Christ Jesus has set you free from the law of sin and death," and in Galatians 6:2, "Carry one another's burdens; in this way you will fulfill the *law* of Christ."

Law-Observing Believers

Biblical faith is evidenced through obedience to God as seen in the first occurrence of faith in Exodus 17:12. Faithfulness is how a follower of Christ lives out his or her faith. Paul exclaims, "The righteous will live by *faith*" (Rom. 1:17). In the same chapter Paul states the reason God called him was to "bring about the obedience of faith for the sake of his name among all the

Gentiles" (Rom. 1:5). True faith is proven by our works and will persevere to the end. Adrian Rogers said, "A faith that fizzles before the finish had a flaw from the first."[106] Basically, if you fail to follow Christ till the end of your life, you may not have known Him from the beginning. When we declare Christ Lord, you and I no longer call the shots; He does. We no longer make the rules; He does. Similar to Zacchaeus and Peter using the title Lord in Luke, we must follow suit.

Christ requires more than lip service. Mouthing the words or going through the motions only works in theatrical plays (or with the former lip-syncing group Milli Vanilli years ago). Kingdom citizenship is proven through action. The words of our Lord should cause us to pause: "Not everyone who says to me, 'Lord, Lord,' will enter the kingdom of heaven, but only the one who does the will of my Father in heaven" (Matt. 7:21). We can't truly voice the words if we aren't obeying the rules. We must respect His authority to know His power.

How do we know the will of God? Was Jesus constantly texting God? Did He send emails non-stop? No. He embodied the Word by hiding God's Word in His heart. If you want to know the will of God, you must know and do the Word of God. Blessing comes in response to our obedience.

When a woman declares one day, "Blessed is the mother who birthed you," Jesus responds, "Rather, blessed are those who hear the word of God and keep it" (Luke 11:28). Jesus is interrupted from teaching with an announcement that His mother and brothers came to see Him. Instead of jumping up to welcome them or pausing His sermon, Jesus says, "My mother and my brothers are those who hear and do the word of God" (Luke 8:21). In speaking on kingdom living, He asks, "Why do you call me 'Lord, Lord,' and don't do the things I say?" (Luke 6:46).

Similarly, Jesus warned His would-be followers against a word-only righteousness: "Not everyone who says to Me, 'Lord, Lord,' will enter the kingdom of heaven, but only the one who does the will of My Father in heaven" (Matt. 7:21). For years, I've viewed this verse through a futuristic lens. But when the verse is "translated back into Hebrew, one recognizes the proverbial form in which there is no real future tense. The saying should be understood: 'Not everyone who says "Lord, Lord" to me *comes* into the kingdom of heaven. . . .' The second part of the verse likewise reflects the idea of present time: 'but he who is doing the will of my Father.'"[107] While Jesus is referencing the Day of Judgment, He is explaining how one's life today is building the case of whether or not they will spend eternity with Him tomorrow.

Ultimately, Jesus reduced the commandments into two categories: our relationship with God (vertical) and our relationship with others (horizontal). He wasn't the first to do this, though. The Talmud, a commentary on the Old Testament, states, "Moses gave Israel 613 commandments, David reduced them to eleven (Psalm 15), Isaiah to six (Isa. 33:15–16), and Micah to three (Micah 6:8)."[108]

Tracks for Life

Our attitude toward the commandments of Christ should be the same as Jesus' view toward the Torah. He loved God's Word. The love of God and the law of God are not against each other. In fact, both are harmonized in the Christian life.

John 14:15: "If you love me, you will keep my commands."

John 15:10: "If you keep my commands you will remain in my love."

1 John 5:3–4: "For this is what love for God is: to keep his commands. And his commands are not a burden, because everyone who has been born of God conquers the world."

A helpful way to view the law differently is to think of it as direction for living. The apostles viewed their submission to the law the same way. Paul refers to himself in his letters as a bondservant of Christ, as do Peter, James, and Jude. Much like the Israelites went from serving Pharaoh in Egypt as slaves to serving God in the wilderness as sons, each understood the Torah to be guardrails or train tracks for prosperous living. God didn't set them free from being servants. He just changed their master. The same is said of us today. We aren't set free from sin to serve ourselves. We are liberated from the taskmasters of sin to serve Christ.

Picture a train derailed off its tracks for a moment. It would appear the train has experienced freedom. It is no longer enslaved. It can finally flourish, right? This visual represents the freedom the world offers. No restrictions, no restraints, no rules, and no regulations. Indulge in whatever you want, whenever you want. "Eat, drink, and be merry for tomorrow we die." This is what the world calls freedom, but it's actually imprisonment. Without a track, the train is derailed and unusable.

Now picture another train on its tracks. It has justification, purpose, and meaning. The tracks provide restraints so the train can fulfill its objective. Instead of holding the train back, the tracks actually give the train somewhere to go. Without the tracks, the train is at best aimless, at worst, wrecked. The tracks are freedom. They are not bondage; they are liberation. Trains only find their freedom within the restraints of the tracks, nowhere else. By the way, the track, or path, that Jesus calls us to walk on is narrow (Matt. 7:14).

The same is true for us as people of God. We find our freedom within the restraints of Christ's commands to love God and to love others. We don't obey the commands out of duty or drudgery. We follow Jesus' instruction out of love and devotion.

Kingdom blessings are received not achieved. Our kingdom standing is a gift from God. "The people of God," cites John Bright, "are summoned to the side of God's Kingdom in the cosmic struggle, but they cannot produce the Kingdom in terms of their own activity." We don't enter it through fighting, struggle, or strength. The author of Hebrews reminds us, "Therefore, since we are *receiving a kingdom* that cannot be shaken, let us be thankful" (Heb. 12:28). We don't receive once and then we are good from that moment forward. It's a continual surrendering of oneself to receive more and more of God.

CHAPTER 10

How Then Shall We Live?

According to the Sages of Israel, the garden of Eden was considered to be a Temple or a sanctuary for God to dwell.[109] The prophet Ezekiel referred to Eden as the Temple, "the holy mountain of God" (Ezek. 28:14). It was a perfect picture of harmony between God and His creation.

God's presence "as a picture in Revelation 21–22 fulfills the mission given in Genesis 1–2, and the progress of this mission can be traced throughout the entire Bible," argue Beale and Kim. They go on:

> In Genesis 1–2, Eden is the dwelling place of God, and God commissions Adam and Eve to expand the boundaries of that dwelling place to fill the earth (Gen 1:28). . . . Mission does not begin with the Great Commission of Matthew 28:18–20, but mission is God's heartbeat from Genesis 1 until the new heaven and earth become the dwelling place of the Lord God Almighty in Revelation 21–22. This ultimate picture of the whole earth filled with God's

presence fulfills God's original intention from
the sanctuary of Eden. We begin, therefore,
with Eden.[110]

Not only does wedding language bookend the Bible (Genesis
2 and Revelation 20); God's presence among His people does as
well.

God patterned the type of routine He expected Adam to follow in how He created the world. God didn't need to rest on the
seventh day, but He knew man would. Adam was given a job in
the garden to serve the Lord by working the ground. His work
was his worship to God. James Hamilton reveals the importance
of living a set-apart life as vessels of God's glory in his book,
God's Indwelling Presence: "In the Temple, Yahweh was present
with His people. He had promised, 'I will dwell among the sons
of Israel' (1 Kings 6:13). Just as God's presence in the tabernacle
had a sanctifying influence on the people, God's presence in the
Temple would incline the people toward obedience."[111]

We prove our allegiance to the King by our obedience
to His commands. Our response to the marriage agreement,
our salvation in Christ, is obedience. God redeems in order to
reveal Himself to reign or rule over His people. That's why the
six-month relocation from Egypt through the Sinai wilderness
took forty years. God didn't place them on an Amtrak train to
Canaan because He needed to reveal His character to them and
outline His expectations. God didn't just have to get the people
out of Egypt; He had to get Egypt out of them. God didn't want
to be just their Savior. He wanted to be their king.

Robert Lindsay, leader of the Baptist Mission to Israel in
Jerusalem, believed that entering the kingdom "was a spiritual
term meaning the rule of God over a person who keeps or
begins to keep the written and oral commandments."[112] When

Abraham, Moses, and the nation accepted the yoke of the covenant of God, they "entered the kingdom of God." By using the yoke illustration, the audience envisions two animals (usually oxen) joined together to accomplish a task by subjecting to each other. Commonly used to describe submitting oneself to the Torah, Jesus encourages His followers to take on His yoke (enter His kingdom) for the burden is easy and the load is light.[113] By offering this invitation, Jesus is contrasting the yoke of the Pharisees, who added "extra" regulations on how to keep the law, with his yoke which is "easy and light."

The Kingdom Advances as We Obey the King

Ferguson summarized kingdom citizenship as belonging "to the people among whom the reign of God has already begun. . . . Where he reigns, there the kingdom of heaven is already present."[114] How does God rule and reign over our life as king? When we obey His commandments and follow His ways, the kingdom advances. We make disciples the same way. Jesus' final words "teaching them to *obey* all I've commanded them" encapsulates that. (For a list of the commands of Christ, see Appendix 1).

Disobedience is common when believers fall out of fellowship with Christ, which is why repentance is necessary. Both Jesus' and John the Baptist's first messages were, "Repent! The kingdom of heaven is here." Repentance is from the Hebrew word *teshuva*, "to turn around or change direction or purpose." The Greek word *metanoia* implies a change of heart or thought that leads to a change in direction. This inner change leads to an outward change of lifestyle. Two clear examples are found in Acts 11:21, "The Lord's hand was with them, and a large number who believed turned to the Lord," and 1 Thessalonians 1:9, "For they themselves report what kind of reception we had from you: how you *turned to God from idols* to serve the living and true God."

During the medieval era, the leaders of the Catholic Church incorrectly interpreted the Greek word *repentance* as "do penance." This is why as a child I grew up confessing my sins to a priest before reciting a list of Hail Mary's and Our Fathers on my knees in proportion to the severity of the sins offered or the forthrightness of my confession. This works-based response to sin is an alien concept in the New Testament.

Turning Around

Don't misconstrue repentance as a work leading to salvation. It's a response to God's grace extended toward us while "we were still sinners." Repentance is a gift as seen in 2 Timothy 2:25, "Perhaps God will grant them repentance." God acted, and we reacted. Change of direction from one's sin is the result of a change of mind over one's sin. As the Word of God is read or preached, we get a sense of God's expectation or standard for our life. Realizing that we are incapable of meeting the righteous requirements of the law, we understand our need for a Savior who accomplished what we were incapable of. Faith, the other side of the coin of conversion, is placing our life in Jesus' hands to save us. Thought of mind is intertwined with change of direction. Without a course-correction in one's life, repentance is reduced to mere remorse, where a person is sorry for getting caught but not interested in changing. An old Cajun preacher on the bayou summarized repentance this way, "I'm sorry for my meanness, and I ain't going to do it no more."

I know I'm dating myself here, but do you remember the movie *Speed* with Keanu Reeves and Sandra Bullock? (It came out my senior year of high school.) A large portion of the movie focuses on the adrenaline-filled runaway bus scene. The bus was filled with explosives that were set to ignite if the bus slowed down too much. Law enforcement realized that the bus couldn't be stopped, only steered in another direction. Our life is similar in that it can't be stopped from moving forward, only altered in the direction it is going. Everyone is either walking toward God or away from Him. We are either growing closer to Him or drifting away. Our direction is an either/or not a both/and.

Repentance didn't disappear after salvation. It wasn't just a one-time act to enter the kingdom. A kingdom citizen makes course-adjustments along the way to experience kingdom living. A person can be a citizen of the kingdom and, at least temporarily, miss the blessings and benefits of the kingdom because of unrepentant sin."

Repentance occurs when confession of sin is present. "If we confess our sins, he is faithful and righteous to forgive us our sins and cleanse us from all unrighteousness" (1 John 1:9). Dietrich Bonheoffer in his book, *Life Together*, believed that "confession of sin is part of discipleship." He said, "He who is alone with his sin is utterly alone. . . . But it is the grace of the gospel, which is so hard for the pious to understand, that confronts us with the truth and says: You are a sinner, a great, desperate sinner; now come as the sinner you are, to the God who loves you."[115] Similar to a front-end alignment on your vehicle, our lives need to be realigned with the Bible or Word of God through confession of sin and submission to the King. Repentance is so important that Jesus spoke the same message to five of the seven churches in Revelation: "Repent!"

Repentance admits that God is in control and we are not. In the context of our topic, repentance is relinquishing control of being the king sitting on the throne of your heart and acknowledging Jesus as King over your life.

Knowing Is Doing

Kingdom living is the outflow of a right relationship with Christ. We glorify King Jesus as we live for Him through obeying His Word. But as Scripture teaches, knowledge precedes doing. John was combating casual Christianity, or cheap grace as it's called today, in his first epistle: "This is how we know that we know him: if we keep his commands" (1 John 2:3). John uses the word knowledge thirty times in this letter alone. He doesn't envision an intellectual checklist of filling the mind with biblical information. John has in mind a personal, experiential knowing of someone intimately similar to the relationship of a husband and a wife. This type of knowledge cannot be learned in school or by completing a course. It comes through experience.

The first occurrence of the word is found in Genesis 4 to describe the sexual oneness of a husband and wife. "Adam knew Eve his wife, and she conceived and bore Cain" (Gen. 4:1 ESV). When Jesus asserted, "You will know the truth, and the truth will set you free" (John 8:32), He didn't pass out a syllabus with course assignments and lecture notes for study. He lived His life before them. Biblical growth, therefore, comes through a deep, personal relationship with Jesus. Before departing this Earth, Jesus explained to Thomas, "I am the way, the truth, and the life" (John 14:6). Truth is in Him.

Therefore, in order to obey the King, we must know what's expected from Him. John is simply repeating what he heard Jesus state in John 15. Warren Wiersbe points out that Jesus taught that the secret of obeying Him is loving Him (John 15:9–10), and the secret of loving Him is knowing Him (John 15:15). "It all begins with your knowing Christ in a deeper way."[116] Love is displayed in action. In the Eastern culture, saying "I love you" was not as meaningful as showing that you loved someone. Now we understand why James says, "But someone will say, 'You have faith, and I have works.' Show me your faith without works, and I will show you faith by my works" (James 2:18). Inward allegiance was displayed through outward action. Even the demons have faith, as James continues. The demons were the first to recognize and identify Him, they tried to break Him, they tried to tempt Him, and they tried to sidetrack Him. Why? They knew He was the Messiah, but they didn't bow down to worship and serve Him. Obedience to God is not a category in their nature.

Obedience, or the lack thereof, reveals one's spiritual condition. Salvation is more than getting answers correct on a spiritual questionnaire or saying "amen" at the right places in a counseling session at the altar during the invitation. Mark Dever lamented in a sermon I heard years ago, "One of the most painful tasks pastors face is trying to undo the damage of false converts who have been quickly and thoughtlessly assured by evangelists that they are indeed Christians."[117] After a revivalist preached years ago, someone who attended the conference and witnessed the influx of people who came forward during the response time asked him: "How many were saved?" The preacher responded, "We will know more in six months." A person who perseveres to the end proves the decision they made was genuine at the beginning of their Christian life.

Rebirth happens in a moment, but our salvation is lived out over a lifetime. True kingdom citizens will reside under the rule and reign of the King as John clearly states, "The one who says, 'I have come to know him,' and yet doesn't keep his commands, is a liar, and the truth is not in him" (1 John 2:4). "Doesn't keep" is the operative phrase in this declaration. It is a present, active verb signifying a long-term, continual rebellion against God. The meaning comes from the maritime world where sailors would use stars to keep their course by looking at the stars at night ("keeping the stars"). Similarly, a follower of King Jesus keeps his or her course by fixing their eyes upon Jesus as they observe the commands of Christ for direction and guidance.

John is not suggesting sinless perfectionism or living a perfect life, for the active tense of the word proves otherwise. These sin practitioners live in sin and love to sin. They are unable to keep the commandments because they don't "know" the King. Paul lists similar actions of lost people who are unable to inherit the kingdom of God:

> Now the works of the flesh are obvious: sexual immorality, moral impurity, promiscuity, idolatry, sorcery, hatreds, strife, jealousy, outbursts of anger, selfish ambitions, dissensions, factions, envy, drunkenness, carousing, and anything similar. I am warning you about these things— as I warned you before—that those who practice such things will not inherit the kingdom of God. (Gal. 5:19–21)

Some have used Paul's words here to support the idea of losing one's salvation.[118] That argument is disarmed, however, with a simple word study of the Greek word *prasso,* translated here as "practice." The word speaks of a repeated or continuous action, similar to the previous usage of the word *keep* in John's epistle. Practicing, in this context, refers to the pattern of one's life—the whole of a person's actions—rather than a single, isolated act. It is the continued, habitual, remorseless practice of sin that identifies a person as having never genuinely repented and been saved. I cannot emphasize this enough: you do not work *for* salvation, you work *from* salvation!

After entering the kingdom, your desire for godliness will increase; your passion for the lost will grow; your time in the word will flourish; and your prayer life will be more intimate as you walk with Christ. You should look more like Christ today than yesterday, or last month, or last year. Don't hear what I'm not saying, though. Believers will battle sin their entire Christian life as evidenced by Paul's own personal struggle in Romans 7:14–23. Believers are not immune from the effects of sin; however, we will not remain in habitual sin without conviction or consequences.

Joseph Frankovic describes kingdom living: "Entering the kingdom of heaven goes beyond piety, uprightness, kindness, and generosity. It cannot be contained within the walls of an institution or adequately expressed by the dogma of a community. It requires subscribing to a new economy that is sustained by God's provision and not material wealth. Those who participate in this economy have joined a movement whose values are inverted, whose agenda is transparent, and whose hierarchy is horizontal. Not many enter the kingdom of heaven."[119] Jesus reminded His disciples, "If you continue in my word, you really are my disciples" (John 8:31). Notice it's not following for a season and then falling away. It's obedience for a lifetime.

Conduct of Believers

This "kingdom gospel" can also be labeled the "discipleship gospel," as Bill Hull and Ben Sobels suggest in their book *The Discipleship Gospel*. "At the heart of the gospel of the kingdom is the question, 'Are you doing the will of God?' . . . Living in the kingdom is the same as being a disciple of Christ, someone who does the will of God."[120]

Discipleship, then, becomes optional when our kingdom focus is only on the future. In this construct, salvation is essential, but following Jesus becomes optional. What good is it to grow in one's faith? What good is it to develop as a believer? Why should I attend church, give, or go with the gospel if, regardless of what I do, I receive a spot in heaven one day? "For almost everyone today in Western Christendom," suggests Willard, "being saved has nothing essentially to do with transformation."[121] Yes, heaven is waiting for born-again believers with open arms, but what about enjoying the benefits of heaven today? Jesus promised an "abundant life" for all who would come after Him. Most certainly, Jesus envisioned a present reality.

Christians should be a people who proclaim the message of the kingdom, display the character of the kingdom, pray for the extension of the kingdom, and walk in the benefits of the kingdom. Every morning believers should experience two acts: a funeral and a coronation. We die to self (funeral) and acknowledge Christ as king (coronation). Remember, we don't "make Jesus king or lord of our life." He already is king. We acknowledge Him as king volitionally and conditionally by submitting to Him. Similar to the Israelites at the base of Sinai responding to God with, "We will obey," we must respond daily and live for Him. Now we understand why Jesus instructed His followers, "Seek first the kingdom of God [everyday] and his righteousness [everyday]" (Matt. 6:33). It's no accident that Paul combined God's righteous acts with the coming kingdom: "For the kingdom of God is not a matter of talk but of power" (1 Cor. 4:20).

Naturally, when your Father is a king, your mind tends to focus on the rewards of the kingdom and not the responsibility of your citizenship. We want blessings without the burden. We want righteousness without repentance. We want redemption without responsibility.

As volitional beings, we are given the choice of disobeying God. For years, I, like you, have heard sermons on the existence of God. "The fool says in his heart, 'There's no God'" (Ps. 14:1). However, a closer look at the Hebrew reveals something about obedience, not understanding. The verse actually says, "The foolish declares in his heart no God." In essence, only a fool would say "no" to God. The word *there* in verse one is supplied by the translator. Further examination of the verse reveals *action* over *belief*: "They are corrupt; they do vile *deeds*. There is no one who *does* good" (Ps. 14:1).

"The law," suggests Ferguson, "is not the basis on which we merit salvation, but it does provide a test to distinguish between those who belong to the kingdom of salvation and those who are outside of it. It's the real test of whether we have been 'born again' or not."[122] Thankfully, Jesus summed up every command into two: love God and love one another. By deepening on your vertical relationship with God, you will notice a difference in your horizontal relationships with others. How do I grow closer to the Lord? How do I foster a closer relationship with God? In the next chapter, we will examine the kind of person who thrives in the kingdom of heaven.

CHAPTER 11

Our Role in the Kingdom

Living a Holy Life

Have you ever heard someone tell you something shocking, something so unbelievable that you're only response was, "No way!" or as my friend Dave Wiley normally responds, "Shut up!" The declaration Paul made to the church of Corinth would have garnered the same reaction. People would have been confused after hearing this line, especially Jewish people: "we [born again believers] are the temple of the living God" (2 Cor. 6:16).

Paul had three Old Testament Scriptures in mind when he made this statement:

> Leviticus 26:11–12: "I will place my residence among you, and I will not reject you. I will walk among you and be your God, and you will be my people."

> Jeremiah 31:33: "'Instead, this is the covenant I will make with the house of Israel after those

days'—the LORD's declaration. 'I will put my teaching within them and write it on their hearts. I will be their God, and they will be my people.'"

Ezekiel 37:26–28: "I will make a covenant of peace with them; it will be a permanent covenant with them. I will establish and multiply them and will set my sanctuary among them forever. My dwelling place will be with them; I will be their God, and they will be my people. When my sanctuary is among them forever, the nations will know that I, the LORD, sanctify Israel."

Now we understand why Paul calls the church to live holy lives in the following verse: "Therefore come out from among them, and be separate, says the Lord; do not touch any unclean thing, and I will welcome you. And I will be a Father to you, and you will be sons and daughters to me, says the Lord Almighty" (2 Cor. 6:17–18).

Disciples of Christ are likened to the holiest structure on planet Earth for the nation of Israel. As a result, followers of Jesus are encouraged to live clean lives before God:

1 Corinthians 7:34: "Be holy both in body and in spirit."

Ephesians 1:4: "For he chose us in him, before the foundation of the world, to be holy and blameless in love before him."

1 Peter 1:15–16: "But as the one who called you is holy, you also are to be holy in all your conduct; for it is written, Be holy, because I am holy."

It's not because you will lose your salvation. It's because you will disqualify yourself from usefulness. Holiness is demanded for those who "are the temple of the living God" (2 Cor. 6:16), and they must "go out from their midst" (that is, the midst of the defiled world) and "touch no unclean thing" because they are priests in that Temple.[123]

Cleanliness Precedes Usefulness to the Lord

William Law, in his book, *A Serious Call to a Devout and Holy Life*, sought out the reason so-called Christians lived like the world in their actions, in this case with their language. He concluded they had no desire to live pleasing lives before the Lord. "For let a man," posits Law, "but have so much piety as to intend to please God in all the actions of his life as the happiest and best thing in the world, and then he will never swear more. It will be as impossible for him to swear whilst he feels this intention within himself as it is impossible for a man that intends to please his prince to go up and abuse him to his face."[124]

We abstain from anything that would hinder our relationship with Christ, for He uses clean vessels. Paul instructed young Timothy in this truth right before he was martyred

> Now in a large house there are not only gold and silver vessels, but also those of wood and clay; some for honorable use and some for dishonorable. So if anyone purifies himself from anything dishonorable, he will be a special instrument, set apart, useful to the Master, prepared for every good work. (2 Tim. 2:20–21)

By reading this book, I assume you are a believer who wants to hear the voice of God, be led by the Spirit of God, commune intimately with God, and do great things for God. We can anticipate this happening as we live clean lives before Him. Young people, and most people for that matter, are driven by FOMO (Fear Of Missing Out). They overcome their fears to ride rollercoasters, stand in line for hours to attend concerts, give in to temptation to "experiment" with certain things, or stay up late to binge watch programs for bragging rights of participation.

What if we viewed our Christian life the same way? God can use anyone for service, but the person who is unclean will miss out on the blessings from being used. Let me ask you: Are you living a clean life? Are you in right standing before God? If there is a consistent, persistent sin in your life that is unaddressed, don't let it fester. Ask God to forgive you today. I implore you to turn from sin and walk with Christ now.

The Christ Life

You may think I'm advocating keeping the law as a new form of repackaged legalism. Not at all. In fact, in and of ourselves, we are incapable of keeping the law. C. S. Lewis writes about how we don't attempt to carry out our faith by "trying to carry it out." Rather, "the real Son of God is at your side. He is beginning to turn you into the same kind of thing as himself. He is beginning, so to speak, to 'inject' His kind of life and thought, His Zoe [life], into you; beginning to turn the tin soldier into a live man. The part of you that does not like it is the part that is still tin."[125]

Jesus said, "If you love me, keep my commandments." When we love, we "fulfill the law." Paul exclaimed, "The law is holy, and the commandment is holy and righteous and good" (Rom. 7: 12) before saying, "The law of the Spirit of life in Christ Jesus has set you free from the law of sin and death" (Rom. 8:2). We do not keep the law to be saved; we are able to obey the Lord because we are saved! How does this happen?

How can I walk with Christ, or as Paul says, "walk in the Spirit"? Deitrich Bonhoeffer summed up the Christian life this way: "Salvation is free but discipleship will cost you your life."[126] We did nothing to earn our salvation, but our sanctification requires our involvement. I summarized this concept in my book, *Bearing Fruit*:

> Therefore, sanctification is the process whereby Christ lives His life through us. A distinction must be made between one's status before God and one's standing before God. "A person's status," according to theologian Herman Bavinck, "therefore, does not yet change his condition, nor vice versa. This holds true in the natural but also in the spiritual sphere. Sin is not merely guilt, but also pollution; we are delivered from the first by justification, from the second by sanctification."[127] **We could say that justification frees us from the penalty of sin, sanctification frees us from the *power* of sin, and glorification frees us from the *presence* of sin.** Believers are expected to sanctify themselves in the Lord through the strength and power of the Spirit within each of us. We walk in the Spirit, as Paul instructed in Galatians 5:16, when we allow God to work *in* us and to work *through* us.[128]

Are you saying we must work alongside God? The Bible clearly states, "If you are led by the Spirit, you are not under the law" (Gal. 5:18). "Under the law," as used in Galatians 5, expresses defeat, bondage, and spiritual ineffectiveness, for the law cannot save anyone. Only faith in Christ saves. However, believers are encouraged to work alongside God in advancing His kingdom. Willard corrects the faulty thinking about our involvement in the process of spiritual growth by saying, "Grace is not opposed to effort. It is opposed to earning. Effort is action. Earning is attitude."[129] Paul repeatedly instructed the churches to "put off" your old self and "put on" your new self, and to "train yourself in godliness," and the author of Hebrews commanded the hearers to "pursue peace with everyone" (Eph. 4:24; 1 Tim. 4:7; Heb. 12:14).

The strength for our working, however, comes from outside of ourselves. God provides the ability to accomplish the work He set out for us. Freedom in the Spirit is not a license to sin. I've heard some people say, "I'm free in the Spirit to do as I please. I can lie, steal, cheat, and enjoy all the world has to offer. No one can tell me what to do." Paul told the church at Galatia, "For you were called to freedom, brothers. Only do not use your freedom as an opportunity for the flesh" (Gal. 5:13 ESV). Being led by the Spirit doesn't mean you're free to do as you please. It allows you finally to worship God freely, live a life pleasing to God, experience victory over sin, and enjoy the abundant life Jesus promised.

We do not walk in our power or please God in our own strength. God is working in us as we walk toward Him. Many Scriptures speak of the both/and of this collaborative working of God in us.

> Colossians 1:27–29: "God wanted to make
> known among the Gentiles the glorious wealth

of this mystery, which is Christ in you, the hope of glory. We proclaim him, warning and teaching everyone with all wisdom, so that we may present everyone mature in Christ. I labor for this, striving with his strength that works powerfully in me."

Who is doing the work in Paul's life, God or him? The answer is both. Listen to him share with the churches of Philippi and Ephesus about the synergistic work of the Spirit.

Philippians 2:12–13: "Therefore, my dear friends, just as you have always obeyed, so now, not only in my presence but even more in my absence, work out your own salvation with fear and trembling. For it is God who is working in you both to will and to work according to his good purpose."

Ephesians 2:8–10: "For you are saved by grace through faith, and this is not from yourselves; it is God's gift—not from works, so that no one can boast. For we are his workmanship, created in Christ Jesus for good works, which God prepared ahead of time for us to do."

Ephesians 3:20–21: "Now to him who is able to do above and beyond all that we ask or think according to the power that works within us— to him be glory in the church and in Christ Jesus to all generations, forever and ever. Amen."

Essentially, Paul is saying, "I'm doing it, but Christ is really doing it through me." God works in us to work through us "to

show that the surpassing power belongs to God and not to us"
(2 Cor. 4:11 ESV).

Martin Luther asks and answers poignant questions with
clarity in regards to this sometimes difficult issue in the lyrics to
his hymn, "A Mighty Fortress Is Our God":

> Did we in our own strength confide
> Our striving would be losing,
> Were not the right Man on our side,
> The Man of God's own choosing.
> Dost ask who that may be?
> Christ Jesus, it is He.
> Lord Sabaoth His name,
> From age to age the same.
> And He must win the battle.[130]

Although God demands obedience as a means of thriving in
His kingdom, He gives us the grace for carrying out His commands. We follow a king who extends what He expects.

Walking in the Spirit

A mentor and friend of mine, Tim Lafleur, always says, "The
Christian life is easy or impossible. It's impossible if you try to
live it in your own strength. It becomes easier as you allow Christ
to work in and through your life." What he means is that anything we do for God in the flesh is like filthy garments to Him
(Isa. 64:6). We must yield to the leading of the Spirit so that He
can work through us. It's a difficult concept to understand, but
allow me to cite Scripture where this both/and concept is found:
God working in us to work through us.

As jars of clay, God fills us with His Spirit to accomplish His plan. The extra-ordinary power within us comes from God, not us.

> Now we have this treasure in clay jars, so that *this extraordinary power may be from God* and not from us. We are afflicted in every way but not crushed; we are perplexed but not in despair; we are persecuted but not abandoned; we are struck down but not destroyed. We always carry the death of Jesus in our body, so that *the life of Jesus may also be displayed in our body.* (2 Cor. 4:7–10)

In Paul's personal mission statement, he writes about the strength of God working within him to accomplish His plan.

> God wanted to make known among the Gentiles the glorious wealth of this mystery, which is *Christ in you,* the hope of glory. We proclaim him, warning and teaching everyone with all wisdom, so that we may present everyone mature in Christ. I labor for this, striving with *his strength that works powerfully in me.* (Col. 1:27–29)

It may appear that Paul is exerting the energy to accomplish the task, but it's actually Christ working within him. In Ephesians, we understand that God saves us by grace through faith for us to do something. The good works that He outlined before the world began will be accomplished by His Spirit.

> For you are saved by grace through faith, and this is not from yourselves; it is God's gift—not

from works, so that no one can boast. For we
are his workmanship, created in Christ Jesus for
good works, which God prepared ahead of time
for us to do. (Eph. 2:8–10)

We will be able to perform impossible feats as kingdom citizens for the advancement of the gospel. The power is not ours; it's God's—which is why there is no room for boasting.

Now to him who is able to do above and beyond
all that we ask or think according to the power
that works in us—to him be glory in the church
and in Christ Jesus to all generations, forever
and ever. Amen. (Eph. 3:20–21)

The clearest picture of our striving and Christ's equipping for service is seen in Philippians 2. Salvation is used in this text, not as a future spot in heaven, but as a present reality in a person's life.

Therefore, my dear friends, just as you have
always obeyed, so now, not only in my presence
but even more in my absence, work out your
own salvation with fear and trembling. For it
is God who is working in you both to will and
to work according to his good purpose. (2 Phil.
12–13)

The ministry of the kingdom is not achieved; it is received from God. This concept frees us from attempting to earn or keep our place in the kingdom. Christ secured our place on the cross. We don't have to work for our salvation. We work *from* our salvation. Our motivation is one of gratitude for what Christ has already done, not one of earning earthly gifts. Moreover, our hope is in the ongoing and ultimate fulfillment of God's promises to us in the future.[131] We've already learned how God operates: He redeems, to reveal, in order to reign over us, so that we respond with obedience.

Walking After the Word

We still haven't solidified what it means to be filled with the Spirit. A clue to Paul's intention is found when we compare two sections of Scripture written to two churches both while he is in prison. In Ephesians 5, he encourages the believers to abstain from getting drunk with wine but rather to be filled (controlled) by the Spirit. Next, he explains what a Spirit-filled life looks like. He employs virtually the same formula in his letter to the church of Colossae. Let's compare the two passages.

> And don't get drunk with wine, which leads to reckless living, but *be filled by the Spirit:* speaking to one another in psalms, hymns, and spiritual songs, singing and making music with your heart to the Lord, giving thanks always for everything to God the Father in the name of our Lord Jesus Christ, submitting to one another in the fear of Christ. (Eph. 5:18–22)

> *Let the word of Christ dwell richly among you,* in all wisdom teaching and admonishing one another through psalms, hymns, and spiritual songs, singing to God with gratitude in your hearts. And whatever you do, in word or in deed, do everything in the name of the Lord Jesus, giving thanks to God the Father through him. (Col. 3:16–17)

The two phrases, "be filled with the Spirit," and "let the word of Christ dwell richly in you," are synonymous, for the result is the same: "speaking psalms, hymns, and spiritual songs, singing to God with gratitude and obeying Him in word and deed." A love for reading the Word, sharing the Word, singing the Word, meditating on the Word, memorizing the Word, proclaiming the Word, and obeying the Word is the result of a Spirit-filled life. The attention of our minds and the affection of our hearts will be on following the King and pleasing Him, not out of compulsion but worship. *We must get into the Word until the Word gets into us.*

Some non-Christians view Christianity as restricting their freedom. From the outside, it may seem like the Christian life is a bunch of don'ts. However, we are free to do whatever we desire. I'm free to rob a bank, but I'm discerning enough to understand the bondage I'll be in afterward trying to cover up the crime, go into hiding, and eventually serve time in prison. I'm free to use drugs, abuse alcohol, and live a sexually immoral life; however, I know firsthand that all of this leads to bondage. I'm free in Christ to make any of these choices, but considering the consequences, would I really be free? As Paul reminds us, "If you offer yourselves to someone as obedient slaves, you are slaves of the one you obey—either of sin leading to death or of obedience leading to righteousness" (Rom. 6:16). In other words, as a Christian, you've been set free; so don't go and become a slave again to that from which you've been freed. Elisabeth Elliot said, "Freedom and discipline have come to be regarded as mutually exclusive, when in fact, freedom is not at all the opposite, but the final reward of discipline."[132]

Freedom to sin only enslaves you to the consequences of bad decisions. Real freedom is the choice to live responsibly under

the protective parameters set out by God in His Word. Adrian
Rogers, once said, "I can sin all I want to, but I don't want to."[133]
When we enter the kingdom of God, Christ gives us the freedom
to choose or reject all that He offers. As we yield to the Spirit,
God accomplishes His will through our lives and we experience
the abundant life Christ promised.

Reorient Our Lives around Making Disciples

Kingdom citizens are expected to make disciples. It's not
an optional endeavor; it's expected. When we adopt a kingdom
agenda, our focus in churches shifts from a "come and see" model
filled with programs and activities "at the church," to a "disciple
and deploy" model where saints are equipped for service as
kingdom agents in the world. Pastoral staff members understand
their role is not to *execute* all the ministry duties themselves, but
effectiveness is determined by how well they *equip* and *empower*
their people to join in the work of ministry.

Evangelism and discipleship become two hallmarks of the
church, with each occupying equal footing under the banner of
disciple-making. These two terms are not mutually exclusive.
They are not the same but are of equal value in the disciple-
making process. The filling of the Spirit was not given to reserve
a seat at the heavenly table one day, but to send disciples out for
ministry today. When Jesus breathes His Spirit on the disciples
before sending them out (John 20:21–22), "It is not the bestowal
of life," according to Bruce, "that is in view now, but empowerment for ministry."[134] They embody God's presence now. As
image-bearers, we are sent out with a message to those outside of
the kingdom rule. Empowerment leads to proclamation.

Jesus' ministry was consumed with raising up many disciples who would carry on the message long after He departed. From the outset of the invitation to follow Jesus, He implanted within the men who would come after Him the seed of replication. "Follow me, and I will make you become fishers of men (Mark 1:17 ESV). Three observations can be made from this initial call.

A disciple follows Christ. In the first century, a would-be disciple would seek out a reputable Rabbi to study under. After questioning the student to determine if he had what it took to be a disciple, the Rabbi would issue a call to follow him. Jesus, on the other hand, breaks the mold by initiating a call to follow Him without the customary questioning of would-be disciples. He's the only Rabbi in Jewish history to summon men to follow Him—unqualified, ordinary men at that. Additionally, Jesus' call is personal. The disciples weren't asked to follow the Torah or even God. Jesus invites them to Himself. No Sage of Israel would think of doing this. Aren't you glad Jesus still seeks out men and women to follow Him?

A disciple is formed by Christ. The word *make* is a future promise from Jesus that will happen by His authority. *Become* is another word for "birth" or "come into existence." We can't manufacture spiritual fruit in our life, but we can plant ourselves in an environment of rich soil for growth. Spiritual disciplines such as reading the Word, memorizing Scripture, praying, fasting, silence, solitude, and sharing our faith, accomplish that very thing in our life. Beale is helpful in showing how the Word of God expands in the life of a follower of Christ:

> How then do we multiply disciples? Disciples multiply only as the word of God bears fruit in and through our lives. In Acts, the Genesis 1:28 language of "be fruitful and multiply"

marks the growth of the church: And the
word of God continued to be fruitful and the
number of the disciples multiplied greatly in
Jerusalem. (Acts 6:7; our translation), But the
word of God bore fruit and multiplied. (Acts
12:24; our translation), and so the word of
the Lord continued to bear fruit and prevail
mightily. (Acts 19:20; our literal translation).[135]

A disciple is focused on others. It's interesting to note what
Jesus doesn't say. He didn't promise, "Follow me and I will make
you rich, happy, healthy, wealthy, prosperous, or successful." He
said, "Follow me, and I will make you become fishers of men."
Being full-time fishermen, they knew exactly what He was talking about. Fishing was hard work that didn't always produce a
catch. You cast many times before hauling in a fish.

I know firsthand the difficulties of fishing. I went out almost
every weekend for fifteen months and only caught five fish on
the Old Hickory Lake in my town. To say I was discouraged is an
understatement. The lack of fish didn't discourage me, though,
from going out again. However, I knew I would catch a fish,
eventually. This year, my hard work paid off. I reeled in a 3.5
pound bass. Some may not be impressed with my catch (Kandi,
my wife, wasn't), but after failed attempt after failed attempt, it
was glorious.

Inviting others to enter the kingdom can yield similar
results. Although we may not see people responding, we don't
give up sharing the gospel. The disciple-making process doesn't
end at the entrance into the kingdom though. Remember, *the
gospel came to you because it was heading to someone else.* That's
where the work begins. In fact, baptism is not the finish line of
the journey; it's the starting line.

Evangelism and discipleship are two oars in the same row boat of disciple-making. You need both of them working in harmony to reach your disciple-making destination. Favoring one, at the neglect of the other, will leave you rowing in circles. A church that exclusively focuses on evangelism runs the risk of becoming a mile wide and an inch deep. On the flip side, a church only concerned with discipling people runs the risk of becoming a mile deep and an inch wide. The pendulum needs to remain in the middle. One of the by-products of the mass evangelistic crusades we've seen over the years is that our focus has been on teaching people to share their faith (evangelism), but we have neglected to teach people how to share their lives with others (discipleship). A change will take place when we move beyond a pitch to a process.

First-Century Soul-Winning

The early church drew people to the movement of Christ not through city-wide crusades or door-to-door evangelistic efforts; both would have gotten them imprisoned or killed during those tumultuous days in the Roman Empire. Even their worship services were not necessarily attractive in nature. Offering a seeker-friendly service for lost people to attend was not the focus. There were many reasons for not offering this type of worship gathering, one of which would have been the threat of death. Church leaders instead understood the importance of "equipping the saints for the work of ministry" (Eph. 4:12).

Alan Kreider, in *The Change of Conversion and the Origin of Christendom*, documents how first- and second-century believers evangelized. He states, "If Christian worship did assist in the outreach of the churches, it did so incidentally, as a by-product, by shaping the consciousness of the individual Christians and the character of their communities so that their lives—and their interactions with outsiders—would be attractive and question-posing."[136]

Lifestyle evangelism, where the gospel was on display through actions and attitudes, won lost people to Jesus. Kreider continues, "Christians who could not publicly articulate their faith were aware that the world was watching them. So repeatedly Christian leaders emphasized how important it was that the Christians' lives be articulate and attractive."[137] Believers lived their lives in such a way that the watching world around inquired about their beliefs. Are we living the same way? Do our neighbors, coworkers, and family ask questions about our God because of our lives?

Ultimately, our goal should be to create a church culture where maturity in Christ is normative so that believers are equipped with confidence to live on mission at their workplace, in their neighborhood, and throughout their community. Viewing our jobs as ministry platforms for sharing the gospel is a kingdom shift. How do you view your occupation? How do you view your workplace? How do you view your office relationships?

Our focus, then, shifts beyond a church building one hour a week to the other one hundred sixty-seven hours outside of it. Gospel intentionality is the driving force of our lives. We go to the same places, at the same time, to see the same people to befriend them, not viewing them as projects but friends. We share our life with them so when their life gets difficult, as all of ours do at times, they know who to seek advice from. We use this open door to share our testimonies of life change and our citizenship in the kingdom of heaven.

From Presentation to Process

Krister Stendahl notes the conundrum of our evangelistic appeals: "It remains a fact worth pondering that Jesus had preached the kingdom, while the church preached Jesus. And thus we are faced with a danger: we may so preach Jesus that we lose the vision of the kingdom, the mended creation."[138] In light of what we've learned, what would you say is the good news or the "gospel of the kingdom"?

In his book, *The Best Kept Secret of Christian Mission*, John Dickson offers a summary statement: "The gospel is the announcement that God has revealed His kingdom and opened it up to sinners through the birth, teaching, miracles, death and resurrection of the Lord Jesus Christ, who will one day return to overthrow evil and consummate the kingdom for eternity."[139] Notice the both/and aspect of his explanation. The kingdom has broken into Earth and will be fully realized when Christ returns for a second time to make all things new.

Years ago, I had the privilege of traveling to the Middle East with my father on his first mission trip. Not an easy journey for a first mission trip, but he was a trooper. One city we visited was predominately Muslim, some were extremist. Openly sharing the gospel was prohibited, punishable by imprisonment or death. Passing out tracks, inviting someone to a service, and even attending church services were not options. Ministry was difficult as the few believers plowed through fallow ground. Viewed through American metrics, the ministry would be viewed as unsuccessful. *Outreach* magazine would not report on the salvation and church growth numbers in this town. However, each laborer had joy in his eyes as stories were shared of God's provision to provide for their needs and soften hardened hearts. No one was dismayed or perturbed by the lack of responses. In fact, they celebrated the opportunities they had to meet a need, share a Scripture, or address a situation biblically.

I asked one of the missionaries, "How do you gauge effectiveness in ministry?" Her response caught our team by surprise. I haven't forgotten what she said since that day. "Our effectiveness is not gauged by how many people we save; God does that. *Our job is to move a person one step closer on a thousand step journey to Christ.*" No one makes a decision to follow Christ isolated from their historical time line. God uses the totality of someone's experiences—hardships and difficulties, successes and failures, hurts and hang-ups—to lead them to a saving relationship with Him. If we are blessed to see the miraculous take place as someone moves from death to life, we can take no credit for that. Someone tilled, labored, sowed and watered that seed before that moment, which is why Paul said, "I planted, Apollos watered, but God gave the growth. So then neither the one who plants nor the one who waters is anything, but only God who gives the growth" (1 Cor 3:6–7).

Don't misunderstand me here. We need to keep sharing the gospel with lost people and then call them to repent and believe. I had the privilege of examining the evangelistic invitation extensively during my doctoral studies. My dissertation investigated how to give an evangelistic appeal to lost people.[140] Nevertheless, we shouldn't be discouraged when they don't respond. What should be more concerning is what believers do after they respond to the gospel.

Making converts is not the end goal. Making disciples should be. The mass evangelism movement hijacked the concept and reprogrammed our minds to think it is. The gospel is the good news that leads to salvation, but it's more than a formulaic prayer. McKnight states, "We can be so singularly focused on the personal-Plan-of-Salvation and how-we-get-saved that we eliminate the Story of Israel and the Story of Jesus altogether."[141] It raises the question: Is the Old Testament even necessary to be saved? Do we need to know about figures like Abraham or Moses, David or Solomon, Isaiah or Jeremiah? Our obsession with "getting people saved" may be the reason we have overlooked our role as kingdom citizens today. John Dickson in his book, *The Best Kept Secret of Christian Mission: Promote the Gospel with More Than Our Lips*, summarizes the gospel this way:

- Jesus' royal birth secured His claim to the eternal throne promised to King David.
- Jesus' miracles pointed to the presence of God's kingdom in the person of the Messiah.
- Jesus' teaching sounded the invitation of the kingdom and laid down its demands.
- Jesus' sacrificial death atoned for the sins of the those who would otherwise be condemned at the consummation of the kingdom.
- Jesus' resurrection establishes Him as the Son whom God has appointed Judge of the world and Lord of the coming kingdom.[142]

In this summary, Jesus is not cherry-picked out of His Hebraic culture or God's sovereign time line. He came to establish His kingdom among His people and fulfill the law and the prophets.

Gospel Now

In order to match Jesus' message, we may need to change
how we present the gospel. Instead of asking people if they want
to go to heaven after death, what if we offer them heaven today?
Not "You don't want to go to hell when you die do you?" but
"Don't you want to experience life today?"

What if our focus was on the here and now and not just the
future there and then? When salvation is reduced to a future realm
we fall "in danger of missing the fullness of life offered to us. Can
we seriously believe that God would establish a plan for us that
essentially bypasses the awesome needs of present human life and
leaves human character untouched? Would He leave us even temporarily marooned with no help in our kind of world, with our kinds
of problems: psychological, emotional, social, and global? Can we
believe that the essence of Christian faith and salvation covers nothing but death and after? Can we believe that being saved really has
nothing whatever to do with the kinds of persons we are?"[143] Is it
feasible to think that God would save us as a child for heaven and
disregard the importance of making a difference today?

Dallas Willard offers helpful questions to discern if we are
preaching the full gospel:

> Does the gospel I preach and teach have a
> natural tendency to cause people who hear it to
> become full-time students of Jesus?
>
> Would those who believe it become His appren-
> tices as a natural "next step"?
>
> What can we reasonably expect would result
> from people actually believing the substance of
> my message?[144]

Kingdom Growth Takes Time

Our salvation in Jesus is not a ticket to the heavenly amusement park. It's a summons into the service of King Jesus. What makes the Great Commission so great is the fact that we are co-laborers with God in His mission of making disciples. He enlisted us to partner with Him in advancing the gospel by investing in the next generation of kingdom citizens. As we have seen already, the kingdom is a mustard-seed movement that develops over time in the most unexpected places and through the most difficult environment. In a culture of "have it now" or "have it your way today," we can become impatient when results are not seen early on.

God doesn't rush to accomplish His work. He may not be on our time, but He is always on time. God allows trials and troubles in our lives to conform and mold us into the image of His Son Jesus. He never wastes a hurt in our lives. Miles Stanford, in his book *The Green Letters*, emphasizes the importance of contentment in the kingdom: "A student asked the president of his school whether he could not take a shorter course than the one prescribed. 'Oh yes,' replied the president, "but then it depends on what you want to be. When God wants to make an oak, He takes a hundred years, but when He wants to make a squash, He takes six months."[145] Do you want to be a squash or an oak? Could this be the reason for the second and third soil individuals falling away as seen in Mark 4? Could intentional discipleship have kept them on the path to eventually bear fruit? It couldn't hurt; that's for sure.

You can't microwave spiritual maturity. It takes time. Think of how long it took for God to mold you into the person you are today. Like a crock-pot roast simmering on a low heat, the kingdom grows quickly at times, but other times it's slow. Sometimes kingdom expansion is undetected, as with the ministry of Adoniram Judson. The movement of Christ today in Southeast Asia is the result of years of tilling up hard soil. At the age of twenty-four, Judson left for Burma with a deep-seated passion to see people come to faith in Christ. His convictions would be

> tested for thirty-eight years in Burma, through the loss of two wives, seven of thirteen children, and terrible sickness at sea that led to his death. In the face of constant persecution and imprisonment, he not only finished a Burmese-English dictionary and grammar but also translated the entire New Testament into Burmese. After ten years, he had one church of eighteen believers.[146]

We must employ a long view of life instead of an immediate view. Don't overestimate what can be done in a short period of time or underestimate what God can do over the long haul of your life. Jesus taught us that the Christian life is simple. We enjoy the abundant, victorious life He intended (through obedience) and we help others enjoy the same opportunity (through disciplemaking). We continue taking a long walk of obedience in the same direction.

In the final two chapters, we will examine the greatest sermon ever delivered, the Sermon on the Mount. Jesus' words are more than inspiring words to meditate on. They are truths to live by. Through the years, theologians and pastors have interpreted the Sermon to mean different things. By viewing Jesus' message through a kingdom hermeneutic, we are able to understand His intended meaning back then and today.

CHAPTER 12

Kingdom Living for Today

In 2007, Mary Hance, a reporter who worked for *The Tennessean*, received an email from a man named Stan Caffy. He introduced himself as "the idiot who donated that Declaration you wrote about." When Stan and his wife were combining their households after marriage, many things inevitably had to go. One item that Stan, somewhat of a packrat, found at a thrift shop in Donelson Hills some years before was a replica of the Declaration of Independence. He'd hung it on the wall in his garage, but he wasn't particularly attached to it—it had little to no value to him, so he donated it to a thrift store.

Imagine Stan's surprise when he found out that same Declaration was sold that year to a Utah investment firm for $477,650. It turned out that the document was not a replica at all, but an original copy of one commissioned by John Quincy Adams in 1820. Only thirty-six of the two hundred original copies are in existence.[147]

Too often, people find themselves feeling like this copy of the Declaration of Independence. They feel undervalued and under appreciated. Believers, however, are citizens of a different kingdom. We do not receive our value from worldly standards or from the opinions of those around us; we serve a higher purpose, a bigger kingdom, and a grander King than this world has to offer. The Sermon on the Mount is Jesus' picture of human flourishing. He defines what the good life looks like, or should I say, the God life.

Kingdom Living

The message of the Sermon on the Mount is not just for the benefit of the multitudes, the scribes, or the Pharisees, although they were in the crowd that day. Jesus is speaking directly to the disciples, whom He just called. Unlike modern messages today, the entire Sermon can be read in less than 15 minutes. With succinct words, Jesus describes kingdom living for His followers at the outset of His earthly ministry.

The scene of the Sermon is reminiscent of Moses, the lawgiver in the Old Testament, delivering the word of God to the people. New Testament theologian Chuck Quarles points out, "Moses is not only a lawgiver, but for the Jews he was also their redeemer, deliverer, and savior, a role that Jesus will play for the Jews and the gentiles."[148]

In addition to thinking of the kingdom as a place we go when we die, for many Christians, believers have relegated the kingdom to the millennial reign of Christ at the end of days. Only recently, Christian philosopher Dallas Willard wrote, "up until about twenty years ago, one could not teach kingdom principles for present living without being regarded as preaching a mere 'social' gospel."[149] Jesus' teaching on the Sermon on the Mount paints a picture of what kingdom living looks like. You may be wondering, *Didn't Jesus come to do away with the law,* for

Paul taught in Romans that Jesus was the "end *of the law" (Rom.
10:4)?* The word *end* in Romans 10 doesn't mean "abolish" or
"destroy" but "goal." Paul's point is clear: Christ came to "fulfill"
the law, not abolish it, as we will examine in a moment. At the
time of the Sermon, the Mosaic Law was still in effect, for Jesus
kept it perfectly. It wasn't until His crucifixion and death that He
terminated the "rule of the law" over one's life.[150]

In his letter to the Galatians, Paul suggested that the law was
a *"guardian* until Christ, so that we could be justified by faith"
(Gal. 3:24). Some have translated the word in a Western sense as
teacher, which misses the point. The Greek word is actually made
up of two words, which can be translated as "'child conductor'
or 'someone responsible for the conduct of a child.'"[151] In biblical
times, people would commonly employ a hired hand or a slave to
direct the child's moral behavior and conduct, oversee the child's
activities, and coordinate teachers and tutors for his or her education until they became an adult. The law, then, was viewed as
a defender or protector, not a jailer or governor. D. T. Lancaster
offers a translation of this verse for clarification:

> Now before faith came, we [the Jewish people]
> were [protected] under the law [kept inside], for
> the coming faith [that] would be revealed. So
> then, the [Torah] was our guardian until Christ
> came, in order that we might be justified [i.e.,
> exonerated] by faith. (Gal. 3:23–24)[152]

The law was given to protect the people and watch over the
nation of Israel until the coming Messiah arrived. Hence, by
obeying the letter of the law with his life, Jesus exemplified what
a perfect life looked life, and thus, fulfilled the law's righteous
requirements.

How to Live Today

In a real sense, Jesus is paralleling Moses by ascending a mountain, or hill, not to receive the Torah from God to give to the people, but to give the word to the people as God. Two verses are crucial for understanding the message. The first verse is found in Matthew 6:8, "Don't be like them," reminiscent of Leviticus 18:3, "Do not follow the practices of the land of Egypt." Separation from the system of the world is imperative.

The undercurrent of the message establishes a line in the sand with those who live like the world on one side and those who don't on the other. Jesus delineates separation from the world as He teaches values, ethics, purity, devotion, prayer, worship, fasting, giving, finances, allegiance, commitment, idolatry, marriage, divorce, lust, immorality, maturity, and the lack thereof. The other verse worth noting is Matthew 5:20, "For I tell you, unless your righteousness surpasses that of the scribes and Pharisees, you will never get into the kingdom of heaven." Righteousness, in this context, is "whole-person behavior that accords with God's nature, will, and coming kingdom."[153]

Some of you may be thinking, *Jesus, now You have gone too far. How can anyone's righteousness exceed the scribes and Pharisees?* We've always heard that these groups were in a class all by themselves. They prayed three times a day, fasted once a week, gave generously (and publicly for all to see), and were trained in the Scriptures. Each man was supposed to be a role model for the nation to follow. But Jesus exposes their hypocrisy. On one occasion, Jesus told His disciples, "The scribes and the Pharisees are seated in the chair of Moses. Therefore do whatever they tell you, and observe it. But don't do what they do, because they don't practice what they teach" (Matt. 23:1–3). They know what's right, but don't do it. By constantly confronting them throughout

His ministry, we realize that Jesus despises legalistic actions that miss the heart of the commandments. In essence, Jesus is calling for a righteousness that is fuller than the righteousness they were displaying, not simply actions that seal theological envelopes but a heart change that produces godly-living. The righteousness of the religious leaders was not adequate to enter the kingdom of heaven.

A better way to think of this concept is "not moral perfection but wholehearted orientation toward God."[154] Jesus calls for a greater, different kind of righteousness that supersedes the Pharisees and scribes. He doesn't have certain activities in mind. After all, who could out-perform the Pharisees in keeping the letter of the law? Jesus calls for a heart change that will lead to doing the right things for the right reasons. Their behavior may be righteous, but their motivation is wrong. Ultimately, the heart of the problem is a problem of their hearts.

By mentioning the righteousness or righteous works of the Pharisees and scribes, He is calling them out for missing the heart of the commandments by putting certain "fences" around the law which prioritized ceremonial observances above the weightier provisions of the law. Fences were "additional stringency meant to safeguard a commandment of Torah."[155] The oral law, later known as the Mishnah, was the Pharisaical interpretation of what God expected from the people. Jesus tells His followers to listen to and observe the Pharisees' teaching but don't do what they do (Matt. 23:3). Jesus' concern centered on hypocrisy and misplaced priorities. Some of His contemporaries kept the letter of the law but did not maintain compassion and mercy as the foundation of their efforts to be faithful to God and His Word. This is the reason He begins the next section with this phrase, "You've heard it said, but I say to you." Jesus reorients

His disciples back to the central emphasis of the Mosaic written commandments to show that one violates the law if love does not serve as the grounds for living out the commandments of God.

With this in mind, it's easy to see that exceeding the obedience of the Pharisees and scribes was not difficult when one's heart is right before God through Jesus Christ. Simple faith expressed through obedience was expected. You may be thinking, *Are you suggesting good works as justification for right-relationship with Christ?* By no means! Paul helps us understand what Jesus was trying to communicate in Galatians 2:16: "We know that a person is not justified by the works of the law but by faith in Jesus Christ, even we ourselves have believed in Christ Jesus. This was so that we might be justified by faith in Christ and not by the works of the law, because by the works of the law no human being will be justified." The Bible is clear: meritorious works save no one. So what did Jesus imply? The Pharisees and scribes were meticulous in teaching and keeping the letter of the law, but their hearts had strayed from the intent of the law. They were all talk, but little action accompanied their words. This is why Jesus quoted Isaiah to condemn them: "This people honors me with their lips, but their heart is far from me" (Matt. 15:8). Jesus' righteousness exudes outwardly in the life of the believer because of an internal heart change at the moment of our salvation.

What Jesus is about to do is interpret correctly the Old Testament law and provide a picture of the kingdom life for His followers, one not characterized by force, disrespect, or revenge but by grace, humility, and dependence. "Yeshua [Jesus] challenged the fundamental teaching," according to Arnold Fruchtenbaum, "by proclaiming a very narrow way of righteousness. He said that a person must experience a new birth to qualify for the kingdom. The means of experiencing this new birth was by accepting him as the Messianic King."[156] Those who live out the Sermon on the Mount provide the fundamental evidence for Christ working in their lives. Jesus expected us to live this way. What follows are the marks of kingdom citizens.

With this in mind, let us listen to Jesus explain what the ideal character of a disciple looks like. The Sermon and the ensuing narrative that follows is bookended with Jesus preaching on the "kingdom of heaven" (Matt. 4:23; 9:35), orienting the reader's focus toward kingdom living.

Attitudes to Be In

Jesus is the voice of authority. The Sermon on the Mount is unlike a presidential address, a commencement speech, or a pep rally. His voice spoke the universe into being and is now explaining what it is like to live as a citizen of His kingdom.

The first part is commonly referred to as the Beatitudes and is concerned with two things: your relationship with God, and your relationship with the people around you. Each of His sayings begins with the word *Blessed* or *Happy,* which has been translated through the years as being fully and completely satisfied, even if things seem unsettled around you. These words fall short of the intended meaning. Jonathan Pennington, in his groundbreaking commentary, sheds light on the intended meaning of the word at the time of the Sermon. By beginning with the word *makarios* (the Greek word we translate "blessed"), Jesus is pronouncing "a certain way of being in the world [that] produces human flourishing and felicity."[157] Instead of using the word *blessed*, he suggests we insert the word *flourishing*. His reasoning is simple: "The first is a statement (in English) that indicates active, divine favor; the second is a macarism [from the word *makarios*], a declared observation about a way of being in the world."[158]

This concept is found in Psalm 1 where the flourishing/blessed individual meditates on and obeys the Word instead of being influenced by the world. The reader is not merely offered a description of what life should be like but an invitation to live this way, motivating one to aspire to this lifestyle. Ellen Charry, in her book *God and the Art of Happiness*, states that most of God's commands in the Bible are not just "voluntarist" but tied to the motivation for one's own well-being or benefit.[159]

With this being said, the Sermon on the Mount is Jesus' offer to a different kind of life. Before we can appreciate the word *makarios*, we must reprogram our minds away from thinking about divine favor and move toward human flourishing or prospering.

The Beatitudes are attitudes to be in. These attitudes are the result of people who are already in the kingdom, not people earning a spot in the kingdom. We are not rewarded for placing ourselves in this spiritual state, for our state is a result of God's gracious invitation into the kingdom. Moreover, believers living in the kingdom are in a blessed state as a result of their salvation. Jesus rights wrong assumptions that people who are wealthy, powerful, and prideful are blessed. By presenting a radical shift in thinking of unlikely circumstances, hearers are left to discern what a "blessed life" looks like. In his commentary on Matthew, R. T. France summarizes the blessed person as "someone who, because of a heart for God, is promised and enjoys God's favor regardless of that person's status or countercultural condition."[160]

One historian noted that the Sermon on the Mount is "neither righteousness, nor yet the new law (if such designation be proper in regard to what in no sense is a Law), but that which was innermost and uppermost in the Mind of Christ—the kingdom of God. Notably, the Sermon on the Mount contains not any detailed or systematic doctrinal, nor any ritual teaching, nor yet does it prescribe the form of any outward observances. . . . Christ came to found a kingdom, not a School; to institute a fellowship, not to propound a system. To the first disciples all doctrinal teaching sprang out of fellowship with him. They saw him, and therefore believed."[161] The Bible never sets a standard for us to live up to in the promise of blessings for a job well done. Instead, we are invited into a running narrative of kingdom living as God outlines what mature, faithful living looks like for believers.[162] As you will see, the Sermon begins with *being* and ends with *doing*.

Impoverished in Spirit

> *Blessed are the poor in spirit, for the kingdom of heaven is theirs.* (Matt. 5:3)

As already stated, the following sayings are "descriptions and commendations of the good life."[163] When Jesus says "poor in spirit," He is not referring to monetary poverty. He's not insinuating that those who are poor are blessed and those who are rich are cursed. He is talking, instead, about spiritual withdrawals from a heavenly bank account. He describes those who are dependent upon Him because of the consciousness of their own depravity.

The kingdom citizen never forgets that he or she was once dead in sin, actively practicing unrighteousness, seduced by the world, enslaved by Satan, and an object of God's wrath prior to coming to Christ. Remaining poor in spirit happens when we recognize what our spiritual condition is separate and apart from Christ which drives us to a healthy dependence upon Him for all things.

Sorrowful over Sin

> *Blessed are those who mourn, for they will be com-*
> *forted.* (Matt. 5:4)

When you live in the kingdom of heaven, you develop a sen-
sitivity to your own sin which produces godly sorrow. Those who
are poor in spirit, recognizing their own condition in the light of
God's standard, are conscious of the ways they fall short of God's
glory—and then weep over it.

Sadly, some preaching today makes sin out to be a bump in
the road, a minor setback in life. Some preachers even avoid the
topic altogether.

When we omit sin from the gospel, there is no need for a
Savior. If you don't think you're that bad, you won't look for
someone to free you from sin's bonds. After being confronted
with their own sinfulness, biblical men and women expressed
consistent brokenness. Isaiah admitted that he was "ruined" (Isa.
6:5); Peter cried, "Go away from me, because I'm a sinful man,
Lord!" (Luke 5:8); Job called himself "vile" (Job 40:4 KJV); and
Paul labeled himself a "wretched man" (Rom. 7:24). If we don't
understand how bad we are, we will never realize how good
Jesus is and how much we need Him. Sorrow over sin leads to
repentance.

Surrendering Themselves

> *Blessed are the humble, for they will inherit the*
> *earth.* (Matt. 5:5)

Kingdom occupants who possess a right attitude of self and
a proper response to sin will submit to God's rule and reign over
their life. Jesus called this "meekness" in the Beatitudes, which
translates as total submission to God. The kingdom of God

reigns supreme in the hearts of the meek because they are selfless, as opposed to selfish. It is the selfless who will inherit the earth.

Meekness does not equate to weakness, for Jesus was referred to as mild and meek. Former pastor of the Westminster Chapel, Martyn Lloyd Jones, proposed that being meek means "we no longer protect ourselves, because we see there is nothing worth defending."[164] We realize our identity is not in self but in Christ. Spiritual brokenness, therefore, becomes the path to spiritual blessedness, and it comes from seeing yourself honestly.

Seeking the Savior

> *Blessed are those who hunger and thirst for righteousness, for they will be filled.* (Matt. 5:6)

A final characteristic of kingdom living is one's hunger and thirst for righteousness. Thirsting for righteousness is the opposite of seeking after what the world offers. Our desire should be freedom from sin and a right relationship with God by living according to His standard. Sinclair Ferguson states,

> Christians are not antinomians, living morally loose lives. They hunger and thirst for righteousness, for a righteousness surpassing that of the Pharisees and teachers of the law. . . . If a life conformed to God's law is God's intention for man, then when we are restored to fellowship with him and live in his will (which is what salvation involves), we will begin to fulfill his intention.[165]

A thirst for righteousness does not come from within but from recognizing what you lack. Our two boys love to snack on junk food. In fact, we call our youngest "Big P" because he sneaks in the *pantry* so often. They get it from me. My mom used to say, "Robby eats us out of house and home," whatever that means. My boys' bad snacking habits got so bad that we had to put a latch on the pantry door to keep them out. As you can imagine, they adjusted to the new security measures with open arms. That's a joke. Every night was filled with begging and pleading for fruit roll-ups, gummy bears, or chocolates. Neither stopped complaining until the latch was undone and the door was opened.

What if we desired righteousness with the same fervency as my boys seeking a sugar high? What if we sought after a right relationship with God with that intensity? Once our overwhelming desire becomes a thirst for the righteousness of Christ, our relationship with God and with those around us will forever be changed.

Our Relationship with Others

When God's people live as citizens of heaven, there are going to be repercussions. When we live for Him, we can expect to be persecuted for it. Jesus never promised an easier life He promised an *abundant* life. Abundance is not measured by health, wealth, and prosperity alone, but by the reward that comes from embodying the teaching of Jesus. Living as kingdom people among other kingdoms means that believers will do four things: extend compassion, experience God, express peace, and experience persecution.

Extend Compassion

> *Blessed are the merciful, for they will be shown mercy.* (Matt. 5:7)

Extending mercy, or compassion, to others means that we respond to their needs. If grace is getting something good that we don't deserve, mercy is sort of the opposite. Mercy is not receiving the punishment we deserve.

Citizens of God's kingdom have received mercy of the highest order, so mercy should be extended in every area of our life. The identifying marker of a person who has received mercy is his or her willingness to extend it to others—*particularly* those who don't deserve it.

We forgive quickly. We extend mercy generously. We love the unlovable. We force hatred out of our hearts and fill it instead with compassion, knowing there is a reciprocal principle at work. Paul encouraged the church at Ephesus to "let all bitterness, anger and wrath, shouting and slander be removed from you, along with all malice. And be kind and compassionate to one another, forgiving one another, just as God also forgave you in Christ" (Eph. 4:31–32).

Experience God

> *Blessed are the pure in heart, for they will see God.*
> (Matt. 5:8)

Purity carries the idea of being unmixed, or without impurities. Therefore, the pure-in-heart have undivided motives. The kind of purity Jesus is referring to comes after faithful self-examination. Believers have identified and understood the wickedness of their own hearts and have relied on the power of the Holy Spirit to seek holiness. In other words, purity is the result of a right response to the gospel.

Perhaps the reason you are having difficulty seeing God work in your life is because your motives are impure. Your heart needs to be cleansed by Jesus' blood. Maybe you need to cry out to God like David did: "Create in me a clean heart!" (Ps. 51:10 KJV).

Though it is true nobody has ever seen God and lived (1 John 4:12), we do witness His handiwork on display. We can experience His goodness. We can sense His presence all around us. Most importantly, we can see God by seeing the Son. Jesus said in John 14:9 that if you have seen Him, you've seen the Father. Through a relationship with Christ, we see the character, compassion, longsuffering, and instruction of God.

If you want to know what God is like, look to Jesus. If you want to know how God would love, look to Jesus. If you want to know how God would respond to a situation, look to Jesus. If you want a relationship with God, look to Jesus.

Express Peace

> *Blessed are the peacemakers, for they will be called sons of God.* (Matt. 5:9)

Jesus does not say that "peacekeepers" are blessed; He says that "peace*makers*" are blessed. The difference is crucial: one simply keeps peace, while the other overcomes evil with the advancement of good. One is passive, the other is active. The Christian life is an active one, going out of our way to make peace with all people around us. A better way to understand this is by examining the antonym.

A troublemaker is someone who riles up strife for the purpose of creating turbulence. A peacemaker, on the other hand, does all things for the cause of unity. These individuals do not resort to gossip, backbiting, slandering, or scandal, but instead actively pursue *shalom*: a whole, complete life for themselves and for those around them.

Unfortunately, just because someone extends mercy, peace, and purity doesn't mean they will always experience it in return. The pattern of the world is antithetical to these things. As a result, the people committed to the kingdom of God will experience persecution.

Experience Persecution

> *Blessed are those who are persecuted because of*
> *righteousness, for the kingdom of heaven is theirs.*
> (Matt. 5:10)

On the heels of peace, Jesus talks about war. He wants us to be fully aware of an important principle in the kingdom: peacemakers inevitably cause trouble. When the disciples preached the gospel in Acts, their reputation was that of ones who "turned the world upside down" (Acts 17:6).

"Blessed are those who are persecuted" is something of a paradox. Persecution is being pursued or hunted down to be harassed or mistreated. Jesus is saying that those who are attacked for righteousness' sake are blessed. We're blessed when we're reviled, mocked, or insulted.

There are different levels of persecution—for example, in some countries Christians are persecuted by being systematically eliminated. Their homes are torched and their heads are removed. At the very least, Christians should expect adversity that falls short of what we would consider "persecution." This might look like having their ideas dismissed or being talked about behind their backs. Whatever the case, allegiance to the gospel brings with it resistance. Still others will be slandered on social media. Whatever the form, persecution is the normal part of living as a citizen in the kingdom of heaven.

When you know the Prince of Peace, you disrupt the unbelieving world around you because the kingdom of heaven opposes the kingdom of Satan. We should be relieved by this for two reasons: first, it diminishes the anxiety that comes with persecution. Know that the path you are taking will inevitably invite attacks; don't be caught off guard. Second, it gives us a metric to discern if we are living as members of Jesus' kingdom when we see persecution coming our way. Paul warned Timothy, "All who want to live a godly life in Christ Jesus will suffer persecution" (2 Tim. 3:12). Rejoice when persecution comes, because the founder of our faith was persecuted as well.

Our present kingdom life is the result of recognizing our poverty of spirit, our complete dependence on God's Spirit, and the expectation to live peaceably and meekly in spite of negative circumstances. By seeking righteousness and God's kingdom first, the reality of the kingdom is experienced today in our present lives. "The Beatitudes," according to Benedict Green, "are a summary description of the character of the true disciple; they encapsulate both the kind of person the disciple will be seen to be if he or she faithfully follows the requirements of the Sermon on the Mount, and, conversely, the kind of person the disciple will need to be if he or she is to rise to its demands and to preserve in the right (and narrow) path (7:13–14)."[166] Do you see the attitudes present in your own life?

Our Words and Deeds Make a Difference

Because of the influence that Christians inevitably have on the world around them, some of which He says will be met with hostility, Jesus transitions into an examination of what our influence should look like. As outward-focused kingdom citizens, we honor God as we draw people closer to Him. Jesus now defines the kinds of things Christians are to do, and how they should be perceived by those around them. To do this, He introduces two images: salt and light.

Salt

Like you, I've heard sermons preached on the benefits of salt. Food that spoils could be preserved by packing it in salt in order to slow the process of decay, making meat usable over longer periods of time. Since the earth is rotting away, the church is a retardant to that decay.

In addition to being an agent of preservation, salt creates thirst. Similarly, a believer's life should be something that so reflects the kingdom of God that unbelievers viewing from a distance should become thirsty for the answer believers have. Believers's lives should cause those around them to desire what they have.

Salt also improves the taste of the food it is served with. It spices up a bland dish. This is a picture of what a believer's life should be in contrast to the lives of those around them: the things that we do, the words that we say, the activities we engage in should be welcome seasoning to a world that is slowly rotting away.

Finally, salt stings. If salt is placed into an open wound, the wound will hurt more than it did before, even if the pain is ultimately a good thing (since salt is a natural disinfectant). In the same way, our lives should affect those around us similarly to how salt stings a wound. The presence of salty believers should reduce sin, crime, corruption, and promote honesty and morality. Whether at home, with our extended family, around our neighbors and coworkers, or simply at the grocery store, believers are called to be salt, agents of preservation, who point to Jesus, the source of satisfaction.

All of these examples unpack the benefits of salt, but is that what Jesus envisioned as a takeaway? I'm not so sure. When Jesus asks, "Can salt lose its saltiness?" it's a rhetorical question. Modern chemistry proves the impossibility of this statement. "The point is that it would be bizarre and unnatural for salt to lose its saltiness: if other foodstuffs are or become insipid, they can be salted into palatability, but this doesn't work for the salt itself."[167] It's important to point out that salt in Jesus' day could become contaminated with other minerals to reduce its effectiveness. Jesus makes an exaggerated statement to get His audience's attention. He highlights the uselessness of disciples who fail to obey His word and expand His kingdom by comparing them to salt that loses its saltiness, which is impossible. You're either salt or not. You can't have it both ways.

Light

In addition to salt, Jesus calls believers *light*. Light, as we all know, has different functions worth noting.

First, light *warns* of oncoming danger. At sea, lighthouses alert ships to the presence of a shoreline. At an intersection, lights signal that you should slow down or stop. On the interstate, reflective lights warn you when you are not in your lane. Believers living as light can warn of the dangers that await those not following the way of life God prescribes. They point out to a watching world where the edges are so that they don't fall off of a moral cliff.

In much the same way, light *guides* people in the right direction. Flashing signs invite you in. Lights line the sides of a runway so planes can land safely. Believers lives should reflect signs that flash, "Follow me to Jesus."

Finally, light is meant to be *seen*. If you are in a dark room and somebody lights a match, even if you can't see the match, you notice the source the light is emanating from. The world is a darkened place; therefore, believers should live as beacons of light that are not hidden underneath baskets or in caves, but standing tall against the darkness that surrounds them.

As asked before, did Jesus have these uses in mind, or was He thinking about something else? When Jesus labels believers the light of the world, He is making an emphatic, exclusive statement. "You, and you alone, are the light of the world!" It is coupled with the responsibility to let our lights shine before men—not to cover them up or switch them off.

In the first century, you couldn't simply stop at Hobby Lobby or Home Goods to purchase a lamp. Their lamps consisted of a sauce bowl filled with oil. Normally, there was a floating wick in the middle of the bowl that stuck up above the oil, while lighting it could be tricky at times. If there wasn't enough oil in the bowl or the wick wasn't floating right, it could be difficult to light. Once the light was finally burning consistently, it would be foolish to hide that light under a basket, and so, too, with us. Once Jesus illuminates our lives at salvation, it would be absurd to keep that light hidden from the world. The purpose of light is to shine. Your kingdom life is meant to shine bright.

Keep in mind that our light is not something we produce. It isn't a tool we use to attract attention to ourselves. We are like the moon—a stark, reflective surface off of which the sun's light can be seen at night. Our light doesn't originate with us; it is merely what happens when we reflect Christ.

So the question ultimately then becomes one that is answered with self-reflection. Are you being salt? Are you behaving as a light in darkness or a city on a hill? Are you flavorful and healthy? Do people see better by you, or do they still have to squint? Some of you may be the only lights in your environment. Your lives may be the only Bible someone has read. Unbelievers may not read the Bible, but they read you and me everyday. Kingdom citizens should be salt and light in their homes—both in the way they treat their spouses and children and also in the way they interact with friends and strangers, alike. We are heralds of the new covenant relationship we have with God through Christ.

In order to be salt and light to an unbelieving world, though, we must first deal with the thing that prevents us from being that. We must shine a searchlight on our hearts to uncover sin in our lives, root it out, and take steps to avoid it again in the future.

CHAPTER 13

Kingdom Living for Today: Part 2

According to Jesus, kingdom citizens, because of their submission to His authority over their lives, will fulfill the true law through Christ. This submission is not out of obligation but obedience—an obedience that is initiated and enabled by Christ (see the section on the Christ life in chapter 11). Let us continue our journey through kingdom living in the Sermon on the Mount as Jesus uncovers the meaning of the law in relation to His followers in Matthew 5:17–20. After that, he will provide practical examples for daily living as obedient kingdom citizens in the remaining verses of chapter 5. The final two chapters, Matthew 6 and 7, offer warnings against attitudes and actions that will sidetrack believers from living under the rule and reign of King Jesus.

Destroy or Establish?

We've already covered what Jesus meant when He said, "Don't think that I came to abolish the Law or the Prophets. I did not come to abolish but to fulfill" (Matt. 5:17), but I think it's worth noting again the significance of His statement. The phrase "the Law or the Prophets" was a common way to refer to the Old Testament. Contrary to what some may have thought at the time, His mission was not to abolish or do away with the Old Testament commandments, but He came to "fulfill" them. In the language of the New Testament, this word can be translated as "establish," correctly interpreted, or "complete the intended purpose."

Jesus fulfilled the law and the prophets through His obedience to the commandments of Moses and through the fulfillment of Old Testament prophesy. As commentator John Philips explains, "The Jews counted 613 separate edicts in the Mosaic Law and there never was a single moment when the Lord Jesus did not absolutely fulfill in every detail every commandment."[168] Through His obedience to God in His life and teachings, Jesus fulfilled the Old Testament by bringing God and His purposes into clearer focus. Jesus is not destroying the law; He is redefining how it will function in the new covenant.

While the law and the prophets remain, the function of each will be different for the believer of Jesus. "From now on," cites France, "it will be the authoritative teaching of Jesus which must govern his disciples' understanding and practical application of the law."[169] The standard of conduct we live by is now viewed through the "lens of Jesus' ministry and teaching."[170] Jesus expounds the superior righteousness expected to be a kingdom citizen in His movement, a righteousness expected is granted by God at salvation and lived out by the believer through obedience.

Jesus expects more than just lip service to ensure fire insurance from hell. A person can't just mouth a prayer, check a box on a visitor card, and go back to living life as they always have.

An all-consuming passion to serve Christ is required. Business as usual is done away with. Enacted obedience is proof of true salvation. We are not saved by "good works," but once we are saved, we will do "good works" for God (Eph. 2:8–10).

Dealing with Sin

In the Sermon on the Mount, Jesus takes what was an impossible standard of holiness—upholding the entirety of the law—and raises the bar. He will show how one can keep the letter of the law and miss the intention or spirit of the law. Jesus drills down on the quality of one's actions not just quantity. He says, "You have heard that it was said to our ancestors. Do not murder, and whoever murders will be subject to judgment, But I tell you everyone who is angry with his brother or sister will be subject to judgment" (Matt. 5:21–22).

He applies the same hermeneutical principle to adultery: "You have heard that it was said, Do not commit adultery. But I tell you, everyone who looks at a woman lustfully has already committed adultery with her in his heart" (Matt. 5:27–28).

Jesus is not heaping burdens on us to make our work harder for us; He raises the bar so that we understand two things: how deeply we need Him, and where our sin comes from. Left on our own, we could never be righteous enough to merit God's favor or to earn His approval. We are simply not good enough. The Bible states that "our righteous acts are like a polluted garment" to the Lord (Isa. 64:6). For every moment we don't sin there are countless moments after when we will, even as subtle as looking at someone lustfully.

Incredibly, Jesus identifies the root cause of immorality and offers a means for removing it so that we are freed from eternal punishment.

The Root of Sin

When talking about sin, Jesus rebuts the scribes and Pharisees who attempted to place ultimate importance on the letter of the law, rather than the spirit that is behind it. By thinking the law was the ultimate end, the religious leaders missed the point. Jesus points out how wrong they were by discussing the most serious sins the law dealt with: murder and sexual sin.

In Mosaic Law, both of these offenses were punishable by death. In every case all through Scripture, both of these offenses are heinous offenses against God. If you murder somebody, you replace God as the author and retractor of life. If you commit adultery, your unfaithfulness to your spouse illustrates your unfaithfulness to God.

Jesus' point is centered around the notion that sin is not a condition of your hands or your feet or your ears, but of your heart.

When talking about sexual sin, Jesus' crowd may have relaxed. They might have thought to themselves, "I've never committed adultery before, so I'm good." or "This doesn't apply to me." But Jesus' raising of the bar would have caused them pause: "But I tell you, everyone who looks at a woman lustfully has already committed adultery with her in his heart" (Matt. 5:28). The key is the word *look*. The tense of this verb does not indicate a glance or a peek, but rather the idea of continuous looking, gazing, and intentional staring for the purpose of lusting.

John MacArthur, pastor of Grace Community Church, states, "Looking at a woman lustfully does not cause a man to commit adultery in his thoughts. He already has committed adultery in his heart. It is not lustful looking that causes the sin in the heart, but the sin in the heart that causes lustful looking. The lustful looking is but the expression of a heart that is already immoral and adulterous."[171] The root of sin is not found outside of us, but is inside all of us from birth. David proclaimed, "I was sinful when my mother conceived me" (Ps. 51:5). In response, we must ask God to remove it and set up boundaries to avoid falling into it again.

Removal of Sin

Jesus' advice for dealing with sin was extreme: "If your right eye causes you to sin, gouge it out and throw it away. For it is better that you lose one of the parts of your body than for your whole body to be thrown into hell" (Matt. 5:29). Jesus uses a favored method for expounding a truth, hyperbole—stressing the extreme to accentuate the seriousness of sin.

We should approach our own sin with the same kind of resolve. If we are prone to sin by lusting after images on the Internet, we should remove that temptation from our lives. For example, take the computer out of your bedroom and set it out in the open for everyone to see. Jesus is not advocating removing your limbs (because even if you gouge out one eye or remove one hand, you still sin with the other); He simply means that we should go to great lengths to control ourselves.

Routes to Avoid

Kingdom citizens, enabled by the Holy Spirit, put to death the sinful desires of the heart. Murder can be traced back to anger, adultery to lust, robbery to greed, and so on. So by addressing the desires of the heart, we kill the things that branch off of them: nip anger in the bud and eliminate murder. Excise lust and you eliminate adultery.

As we seek to eliminate sin, we can do two things to help us safeguard against it: killing the desires of the flesh through the Spirit and saturating ourselves with the Word of God.

We can't eliminate temptation from our lives, but we *can* respond to it in a biblical way. If you are aware of the path that sin takes (lust leading to adultery), you can avoid or end it before it takes hold. We must pinch off the hose, stop the blood flow, turn the faucet off, and starve the fire of sin in our lives. It is not enough to be aware of every avenue sin can take, because we will quickly be overwhelmed by the different fronts of its attack; instead, it must be cut off at the source. The Puritan John Owen said, "Be killing sin or sin will be killing you."[172] Ruthlessly eliminate anything in your life that could cause you to fall. Institute healthy parameters for protection.

By saturating ourselves with the Word of God, though, we take away the spaces in which sin festers and grow. Every moment you spend focused on the things of the Spirit is a moment you are less likely to be thrown for a loop by temptation. The only weapon you wield to withstand the evil one is the sword of the Spirit (Eph. 6:17). Saturate your life with the Word and the roots of sin will have nowhere to nestle.

The Heart of the Issue

Jesus continues His discussion of the kind of righteousness that is required to enter the kingdom of heaven by focusing on outward piety. Before diving into the deep end of kingdom ethics, He warns against inappropriate heart motives for the accolades of others: "Be careful not to practice your righteousness in front of others to be seen by them. Otherwise, you have no reward with your Father in heaven" (Matt. 6:1). One author translates "practice" as "performing," which gives greater meaning into Jesus' message.

Notice Jesus doesn't warn against practicing righteousness. In fact, He just encouraged the disciples to "let their light shine before others." Instead, He cautions His hearers against self-serving motives for the applause of men. By doing so, it's as if God doesn't acknowledge one's deeds at all. Good deeds done with improper motives are unrecognized in the eyes of God. Quarles notes, "Jesus did not merely command His disciples to do the right thing; He commanded them to do the right thing for the right reason."[173]

Jesus selected three practices—almsgiving, prayer, and fasting—which established one outwardly as religious, to warn the disciples against falling into this ritualistic trap. Each deals with the motivation of one's heart, and each activity is a deliberate action on the part of the believer. None, as Jesus implies, come naturally. We are to examine the motives of our hearts privately against what we do publicly. The spiritual hypocrisy of the Pharisees is seen in their disconnected relationship with God. In the eighteen verses of chapter six, God is referred to as *father* ten times, implying the leadership of Israel doesn't have that kind of relationship with Him.[174] Instead of a loving father who provided guidelines for living, the Pharisees viewed God as a taskmaster or slave driver. This theme is often overlooked in the parable of the prodigal son. The older brother's reason for not celebrating the return of his younger brother is telling: "Look, I have been slaving many years for you, and I have never disobeyed your orders" (Luke 15:29). Sadly, service to his father was out of duty not devotion. He essentially dissed graced, or dis-graced his dad, something that can happen to us if we are not careful.

God's Kingdom Is All Around Us

Imbedded within the Lord's Prayer is a clue about the present reality of the kingdom. As already noted, God's kingdom expands through our obedience to His will. Our daily prayers remind us how the kingdom expands among us and through us. Without the use of bold, italics, commas, or punctuation marks, Rabbis relied on repetition and reiteration to emphasize their points. When Isaiah enters the presence of the Lord, he hears bellowing angels shouting in an ascending manner: "holy, Holy, HOLY!" Elsewhere, Jesus uses the literary technique of parallelism to teach on the kingdom of heaven: "Your kingdom come. Your will be done on earth as it is in heaven" (Matt. 6:10).

For centuries many believers have prayed this model prayer—you may know it as the Our Father—with eschatological [future] lenses on: Our Father in heaven, your name be honored as holy. Your kingdom come. Your will be done" (Matt. 6:9–10). By doing this, we envisage the day Jesus returns a second time to instate His kingdom once and for all with judgment for the wicked and peace for the saints. While the concept is true throughout Scripture, Jesus does not have that in mind in this text. The two lines are synonymous with one another.[175] They are one in the same. A similar example can be found in Psalm 119:105, "Your word is a lamp to my feet and a light to my path" (ESV). Both lines are synonymous with one another. Therefore, the kingdom of heaven comes to Earth when kingdom citizens live holy and just lives, walk upright, and bless others around them. As God's will is done in our lives, the kingdom comes to our lives. We experience this by submitting to God's rule over our lives.

By praying, "Your kingdom come," we are not only crying out, "Come, Lord Jesus," asking for God's final kingdom to be established in the age to come; we are also asking God to perform more redemptive acts in our midst, heal more people close to us, increase His power among us, and save more people around us. God's kingdom is on display when vessels of honorable use purify themselves to be "special instrument[s], set apart, useful to the Master, and prepared for every good work" (2 Tim. 2:21).

American-born pastor of the Narksis Street Congregation in Jerusalem, Bob Lindsey, likened our prayers to fans cheering on their favorite football team. The difference is that we are supporting the work of Jesus in our lives. "Go, Jesus Go! Break into our lives and take charge. When we submit to you, you cause the blind to see, the lost to be saved, the lame to walk, the deaf to hear, and the devil to be squelched. Manifest your kingdom among us and use me."[176]

Our outward focus on God's kingdom and not our agenda moves us from saying, "What can the kingdom do for me?" to "What can I do for the kingdom?" Allegiance to the kingdom is our first priority. Loving self and neighbor appears after loving God. Seeking first God's kingdom is tantamount to every other goal in life.

Kingdom First Living

Another verse that speaks of righteousness and the kingdom as God's rule and reign over His followers is Matthew 6:33, "But seek first the kingdom of God and his righteousness, and all these things will be provided for you." Interpreting righteousness in this verse as one's imputed legal standing before God, free from any human works, misses the point of Jesus' charge. Jesus summons "behavior that accords with God's nature, will, and coming kingdom. . . . The typical Protestant reading of 6:33 as exhorting people to seek after Christ's imputed righteousness, as true and helpful as this is a broader theological truth, has nothing to do with what this verse is saying."[177] The true disciple of Christ will actively practice righteousness, as the Sermon expects. Practicing righteousness, or performing righteousness as noted, is not wrong in and of itself, as seen by Jesus' own words in Matthew 6:1. The problem, as Jesus states, is when our motivation is to "be seen by men. Otherwise, you have no reward with your Father in heaven" (Matt. 6:1).

The grace of God motivates us to live out our faithfulness toward God. Sadly, many have erred on the side of laziness in an attempt to swing the pendulum away from works or fear of legalism. While we can't earn God's favor, that shouldn't preclude us from striving toward Him. Remember the words of Dallas Willard: "Grace is not opposed to effort, it is opposed to earning. Earning is an attitude. Effort is an action. Grace, you know, does not just have to do with forgiveness of sins alone."[178] One author suggested "salvation by allegiance alone," in place of the word *faith*, to describe our unwavering commitment to Christ at the moment of salvation.[179]

The Kind of Prayer God Answers

Saturating ourselves in the Word is a practice that believers should be regularly engaged in, because it is the Word that initiates transformative work in our lives. In addition to reading daily, we should also be in constant communication with our Father through prayer.

Some have miscategorized prayer as a spiritual Christmas list, as if God is a utilitarian genie who grants requests we ask for as long as we ask a certain way or act a certain way. Some use prayer as a demonstration of how holy they are. They will use impressive words when in public to show off the depth of their own spirituality. They boast about the fervency and frequency of their prayer life.

Then there are others who say, "Why isn't God answering my prayers? Doesn't He hear me? My life is such a wreck. I don't even know if God is even listening." Both of these extremes can be addressed by gaining a correct understanding of what prayer is.

Jesus promised in Matthew 7:7–8: "Ask, and it will be given to you. Seek, and you will find. Knock, and the door will be opened to you. For everyone who asks receives, and the one who seeks finds, and to the one who knocks, the door will be opened." So many times, this text is mishandled and twisted into something like this: "Ask anything you desire and God will answer it!" "Seek anything you want and you will find it!" Some have called it "name it and claim it." If you want a Cadillac, pray for it. If you want a new house, ask God for it. If you desire to win the football game, bow your head before the game. After all, God wants everyone to be rich and happy by experiencing your best life now!

This was not Jesus' intention at all. Jesus doesn't envision prayer requests answered as if Christians simply had blank spiritual checks. Jesus' half brother James stated, "You do not have because you do not ask. You ask and don't receive because you ask with wrong motives, so that you may spend it on your pleasures" (James 4:2–3). Jesus anticipates us praying in accordance with His plan and purpose for our life.

The entire section is about entering and living the kingdom of heaven, not personal requests being answered. Each word—ask, seek, and find—is a command of action, stressing the importance of continual action on our part. All of these are appeals "to a gracious God for entrance into the kingdom."[180] Seek, for example, was used earlier in reference to "seek[ing] first the kingdom of God and his righteousness" (Matt. 6:33). Similarly, a person knocks on a door or a gate, as seen in Acts 12:13 when Peter knocks on the door in the gateway. Commentator Craig Keener suggests that we should "knock at the narrow gate through which one enters the kingdom."[181] Jesus wants His followers to continue to ask, seek, and knock until they experience all the benefits the kingdom of heaven has to offer.

Assurance of Prayer

> "Who among you, if his son asks him for bread, will give him a stone? Or if he asks for a fish, will give him a snake? If you then, who are evil, know how to give good gifts to your children, how much more will your Father in heaven give good things to those who ask him." (Matt. 7:9–11)

Imagine one of my boys coming up to me and asking for a piece of toast to eat. Instead of edible food, I hand him a flat rock that looks like bread. I mockingly say, "Here, buddy, I hope you enjoy it! By the way, watch out—that first bite is a doozy." As he crunches down on the rock and chips his front teeth, I say, "Oh, man! It looks a little stale!"

No father today, or in the first century for that matter, would do that to his child. Similarly, God does not treat us that way. Do not misunderstand Jesus: He does not assure that He will give His children everything they desire. But He *is* saying that whatever He gives will be good. God always gives you good things. He may not give us what we want, but He always gives us what we need. When we pray with God's will in mind, He answers our prayers. As we seek first the kingdom with our lives, our prayers shift from trying to get our will into heaven, toward trying to get heaven's agenda into ours. Our response simply is: "Your will be done!"

Anyone seeking access to the kingdom will be welcomed. Living as kingdom people immediately separates us from the world around us. We will think, act, and react differently than the people who surround us. His people are a separate and holy people, designated not for personal glory, but for magnifying His name in a world that desperately needs to know Him. Consequently, others around us will be attracted to the Lord by our lifestyle.

Hearing and Doing

Sadly, few people will find the path that leads to the kingdom, according to Jesus, but many will stroll on the wide road that leads to death. He says, "Enter through the narrow gate. For the gate is wide and the road broad that leads to destruction, and there are many who go through it. How narrow is the gate and difficult the road that leads to life, and few find it" (Matt. 7:13–14). Jesus commonly interchanges the words "kingdom of heaven" with "life" as seen in the encounter with the rich young ruler (Matt. 19:23–24; 19:17). "Gate" is a designation for entering the kingdom as well as seen in the previous section on praying. Further proof is found in the definite article "the" before gate. Entrance into the kingdom is found in one and only one gate, or as Jesus said to Thomas, "I am the way, the truth, and the life. No one comes to the Father except through me" (John 14:6).

Walking is always a reference to "obeying the Lord." When Jesus summoned His disciples with these words, "come follow me," He expected a life of obedience to His teaching and commands, for to follow a Rabbi meant to obey him.

The evidence to prove kingdom inclusion is one's lifestyle. The fruit in one's life (good works) will reveal the root of one's heart. Even though someone proclaims to be in the kingdom with their lips, it may not translate into how they conduct their lives. Jesus gave a stern warning to His disciples:

> Not everyone who says to me, "Lord, Lord," will enter the kingdom of heaven, but only the one who does the will of my Father in heaven. On that day many will say to me, "Lord, Lord, didn't we prophesy in your name, drive out demons in your name, and do many miracles in your name?" Then I will announce to them, "I never knew you. Depart from me, you law-breakers!" (Matt. 7:21–23)

A day of reckoning is coming when Christ will determine one's allegiance to His kingdom by our obedience to the King. Lip service alone is not enough, for many will profess to be followers of Christ, but their life will prove otherwise. "Doing the will of the Father" was a common rabbinic saying for "obeying the word." As Quarles says, "Jesus was not pitting obedience against faith but was insisting that obedience is the necessary expression of true faith.

The 'will' of the Father is God's moral will as expressed through the commandments of the OT and the teaching of Jesus, especially the teachings of the Sermon on the Mount."[182]

The religious leaders problem was not what they did, but what they said they did. Hollow words may fool you of your eternal security, but "your law-breaking actions," as Jesus states, "prove otherwise." Only obedience to the commands of Christ as the result of salvation is validation for one's salvation.

The real question is not: "Do you know Jesus?" The most important question in the end is: "Does Jesus know you?" If you know Him from a distance but have not surrendered your life to Him, you need to turn in repentance from your reliance upon yourself and place your faith entirely in Him, trusting that only He can save you from the consequences of your sin and bring you to God.

No one wants to stand before the judge of all the Earth and not be known by Him.

> "Jesus, it's me, Susan. I visited church every Easter and Christmas!"

> "Have I met you before?" Jesus asks.

> "Hey Jesus, do you remember me? It's Mike!"

> His reply may be: "Do I know you?"[183]

Jesus quotes Psalm 6:8, "Depart from me, all evildoers," to reveal the fact that He never met them before. When the marriage supper seating arrangement is given out, these individuals will find there is no place at the table for them.

Living in the kingdom as a disciple of Jesus is more than just reciting words at the right place in a prayer (a non-Jewish way of thinking about salvation). True discipleship demands obedience to Jesus. We understand that our lives now belong entirely to Him, and He rules and reigns over our life.

A Wise Man

The entire Sermon about entering the kingdom can be summed up with one word: obedience. Obedience to what? The content of the Sermon on the Mount. The conclusion of the Sermon validates this point by describing the building foundations for two categories of people. Those who disregard the teachings of Jesus will falter with the first windstorm of life. However, those who build their lives on the rock of Christ, the firm foundation of His words, will remain steadfast.

Jesus didn't just encourage His disciples to listen, take notes, or even remember His words. He insisted, "Everyone who hears these words of mine and *acts on them* [obeys] will be like a wise man who built his house on the rock" (Matt. 7:24). It's no wonder that He reiterates this point before He departs for heaven in the Great Commission: "teaching them to *observe* [obey] everything I have commanded you" (Matt. 28:20).

A wise disciple listens and obeys the commands of Jesus, the result of which is blessings from God. The Old Testament promised something similar for those who obey God's commands: "Do what is right and good in the LORD's sight, so that you may prosper and so that you may enter and possess the good land the LORD your God swore to give your fathers" (Deut. 6:18). "In Apostolic teaching," according to D. T. Lancaster, "to 'go in and possess the good land' is equivalent to entering the kingdom of heaven."[184] Similar to how Moses ended the giving of the law with a choice for the people of whether they would obey or disregard the commands of God, Jesus concludes with options for building our lives.

As in the Old Testament, obedience brought blessings while disobedience brought curses. Moses explained, "Now if you faithfully obey the LORD your God and are careful to follow all his commands I am giving you today, the LORD your God will put you far above all the nations of the earth. All these blessings will come and overtake you, because you obey the LORD your God. . . . But if you do not obey the LORD your God by carefully following all his commands and statutes I am giving you today, all these curses will come and overtake you" (Deut. 28:1–2, 15). Expecting the same obedience from His followers, Jesus concludes His teaching in a similar fashion.

We should not think of obedience in categories of working harder in our own strength to become holy. Rather, our mind-set should be similar to the puritan John Owen who wrestled with mortifying the flesh. Tim Keller summarized Owens thoughts: "The root of our sinful behavior is an inability to hate sin for itself and this stems from a tendency to see obedience a s simply a way to avoid danger and have a good life—not as a way to love and know Jesus for who he is."[185]

The entire Sermon encapsulates Jesus' central message: "Repent for the kingdom of heaven is at hand." Jesus is contrasting the difference between "hearing and doing vs. hearing without doing."[186] Darrell Bock summed up the entire Sermon with these words: "Jesus is a figure who is not placing his teaching forward because it is a recommended way of life. He represents far more than that. His teaching is a call to an allegiance that means the difference between life and death, between blessing and woe. Jesus is more than a prophet."[187] Essentially, His words are life that leads to abundant life in the kingdom of heaven here, now, and forevermore.

With a present-tense understanding of the kingdom, in place of just a future one, we should view our lives and ministry differently. Our role as Christians is not a passive one where we sit idly by and watch, but a participatory one of advancing the kingdom by pushing back darkness with light. The Great Commission summons all of us to become gospel co-workers. Our marching orders are the teachings of the Sermon on the Mount. Will the road be difficult? You bet. Remember, Jesus wasn't crucified for following the ways of the world. He lived counter-culturally, and so should we.

Kingdom living should never be boring or mundane, for every day is a new adventure. Stanley Hauweras wrote an entire chapter on this concept: "When we are baptized, we (like the first disciples) jump on a moving train. As disciples, we do not so much accept a creed, or come to a clear sense of self-understanding . . . we become part of a journey that began long before we got here and shall continue long after we are gone."[188] Every day we should arise and ask God to fill us with His Spirit in order to accomplish His purposes through our lives. We should pray God-sized prayers and leave the results to Him.

Next Steps

Knowing what we know about the immediacy of the kingdom of heaven, where do we go from here? Let me offer a few questions to ponder and pray about to spark conversation and action:

- What did I learn about God's kingdom and why does it matter?

- As I reorient my mind toward a here-and-now mentality instead of a tomorrow-and-there perspective, what changes?
- How does this affect the gospel I preach and share?
- How does this perspective change the way I do evangelism?
- How does it alter the way I live my life?
- What deliberate steps need to be taken today?
- How can you submit to the leadership of the Holy Spirit in your life?

The Commands of Christ

The list is not exhaustive but will provide an overview of what Jesus commanded His followers.

Repent

"From then on Jesus began to preach, 'Repent, because the kingdom of heaven has come near.'" (Matthew 4:17)

Follow Him

"'Follow me,' he told them, 'and I will make you fish for people.'" (Matthew 4:19)

Let Your Light Shine

"In the same way, let your light shine before others, so that they may see your good works and give glory to your Father in heaven." (Matthew 5:16)

Be Reconciled

"So if you are offering your gift on the altar, and there you remember that your brother or sister has something against you, leave your gift there in front of the altar. First go and be reconciled with your brother or sister, and then come and offer your gift." (Matthew 5:23–24)

Don't Lust

"You have heard that it was said, Do not commit adultery. But I tell you, everyone who looks at a woman lustfully has already committed adultery with her in his heart. If your right eye causes you to sin, gouge it out and throw it away. For it is better that you lose one of the parts of your body than for your whole body to be thrown into hell. And if your right hand causes you to sin, cut it off and throw it away. For it is better that you lose one of the parts of your body than for your whole body to go into hell." (Matthew 5:27–30)

Make No Oaths

"But I tell you, don't take an oath at all: either by heaven, because it is God's throne; or by the earth, because it is his footstool; or by Jerusalem, because it is the city of the great King. Do not swear by your head, because you cannot make a single hair white or black. But let your 'yes' mean 'yes,' and your 'no' mean 'no.' Anything more than this is from the evil one." (Matthew 5:34–37)

Don't Resist Evil with Evil

"But I tell you, don't resist an evildoer. On the contrary, if anyone slaps you on your right cheek, turn the other to him also. As for the one who wants to sue you and take away your shirt, let him have your coat as well. And if anyone forces you to go one mile, go with him two. Give to the one who asks you, and don't turn away from the one who wants to borrow from you." (Matthew 5:39–42)

Love and Pray for Your Enemies

"But I tell you, love your enemies and pray for those who persecute you, so that you may be children of your Father in heaven. For he causes his sun to rise on the evil and the good, and sends rain on the righteous and the unrighteous. For if you love those who love you, what reward will you have? Don't even the tax collectors do the same?" (Matthew 5:44–46)

Be Perfect (in Love)

"Be perfect, therefore, as your heavenly Father is perfect." (Matthew 5:48)

Seek God's Kingdom First

"But seek first the kingdom of God and his righteousness, and all these things will be provided for you." (Matthew 6:33)

Don't Judge

"Do not judge, so that you won't be judged." (Matthew 7:1)

Don't Give What Is Holy to Dogs

"Don't give what is holy to dogs or toss your pearls before pigs, or they will trample them under their feet, turn, and tear you to pieces." (Matthew 7:6)

Treat People as You Want to be Treated

"Therefore, whatever you want others to do for you, do also the same for them, for this is the Law and the Prophets." (Matthew 7:12)

Enter Heaven Through the Narrow Gate

"Enter through the narrow gate. For the gate is wide and the road broad that leads to destruction, and there are many who go through it. How narrow is the gate and difficult the road that leads to life, and few find it." (Matthew 7:13–14)

Beware of False Prophets

"Be on your guard against false prophets who come to you in sheep's clothing but inwardly are ravaging wolves. You'll recognize them by their fruit. Are grapes gathered from thornbushes or figs from thistles?" (Matthew 7:15–16)

Follow Jesus

"But Jesus told him, 'Follow me, and let the dead bury their own dead.'" (Matthew 8:22)

Ask God to Send Out Workers

"Then he said to his disciples, 'The harvest is abundant, but the workers are few. Therefore, pray to the Lord of the harvest to send out workers into his harvest.'" (Matthew 9:37–38)

Don't Fear Those Who Can Kill the Body

"Don't fear those who kill the body but are not able to kill the soul; rather, fear him who is able to destroy both soul and body in hell." (Matthew 10:28)

Come to Jesus for Rest

"Come to me, all of you who are weary and burdened, and I will give you rest." (Matthew 11:28)

Confront Brothers in Private First

"If your brother sins against you, go and rebuke him in private. If he listens to you, you have won your brother. But if he won't listen, take one or two others with you, so that by the testimony of two or three witnesses every fact may be established. If he doesn't pay attention to them, tell the church. If he doesn't pay attention even to the church, let him be like a Gentile and a tax collector to you." (Matthew 18:15–17)

Forgive Seven Times Seventy Times

"Then Peter approached him and asked, 'Lord, how many times shall I forgive my brother or sister who sins against me? As many as seven times?' 'I tell you, not as many as seven,' Jesus replied, 'but seventy times seven.'" (Matthew 18:21–22)

Render to Caesar What is Caesar's

"Then he said to them, 'Give, then, to Caesar the things that are Caesar's, and to God the things that are God's.'" (Matthew 22:21)

Love God

"He said to him, 'Love the Lord your God with all your heart, with all your soul, and with all your mind. This is the greatest and most important command.'" (Matthew 22:37–38)

Love Your Neighbor

"The second is like it: Love your neighbor as yourself." (Matthew 22:39)

Partake of Communion

"As they were eating, Jesus took bread, blessed and broke it, gave it to the disciples, and said, 'Take and eat it; this is my body.' Then he took a cup, and after giving thanks, he gave it to them and said, 'Drink from it, all of you.'" (Matthew 26:26–27)

Keep Guard Against Sin

"Stay awake and pray, so that you won't enter into temptation. The spirit is willing, but the flesh is weak." (Matthew 26:41)

Make Disciples

"Go, therefore, and make disciples of all nations, baptizing them in the name of the Father and of the Son and of the Holy Spirit, teaching them to observe everything I have commanded you. And remember, I am with you always, to the end of the age." (Matthew 28:19–20)

Preach the Gospel

"Then he said to them, 'Go into all the world and preach the gospel to all creation.'" (Mark 16:15)

Be On Guard against Greed

"He then told them, 'Watch out and be on guard against all greed, because one's life is not in the abundance of his possessions.'" (Luke 12:15)

Invite the Poor

"He also said to the one who had invited him, 'When you give a lunch or a dinner, don't invite your friends, your brothers or sisters, your relatives, or your rich neighbors, because they might invite you back, and you would be repaid. On the contrary, when you host a banquet, invite those who are poor, maimed, lame, or blind. And you will be blessed, because they cannot repay you; for you will be repaid at the resurrection of the righteous.'" (Luke 14:12–14)

Love One Another

"I give you a new command: Love one another. Just as I have loved you, you are also to love one another." (John 13:34)

"This is my command: Love one another as I have loved you." (John 15:12)

"This is what I command you: Love one another." (John 15:17)

APPENDIX 2

Priests of the Old Testament

High Priests from 1560 BC to 172 BC

Aaron

Eleazar

Phinehas

Abishua

Bukki

Uzzi

Eli

Ahitub

Ahijah

Abimelech

Abiathar

Zadok

Ahimaaz

Azariah

Joran/Joash

Jehoiarib

Axiomar/Jehoshaphat

Jehoiada

Phidea/Pedalah

Sudeas/Zedekiah

Azariah

Jotham

Uriah

Azariah

Odeas/Hoshaiah

Shallum

Hilkiah

Azariah

Seraiah

Jehozadak

Joshua

Joiakim

Eliashib

Joiada

Jonathan

Jaddua

Onias

Simon the Just

Eleazar

Manasseh

Onias II

Simon II

Onias III

High Priests from 172 BC to AD 70

Jason

Menelaus

Alcimus

Noathan

Simon the Prince

John

Aristobulus I

Alexander Jannaeus

Hyrcanus I

Aristobulus II

Hyrcanus II

Antigone

Hananeel

Aristobulus III

Jesus, son of Phabet

Simon, son of Boethus

Mattathias

Joazar

Eleazar, son of Boethus

Jesus, son of Sie

Ananus

Ismael

Eleazar, son of Ananus

Simon, son of Camithus

Joseph (called Caiaphas)

Jonathan, son of Ananus

Theophilus, son of
  Ananus

Simon, or Cantheras,
  son of Boethus

Mattathias, son of Ananus

Eiloneus, son of
  Cantheras

Joseph, son of Cainus

Ananias, son of Nebedeus

Ishmael, son of Fabi

Joseph, son of Simon

Ananus, son of Ananus

Jesus, son of Damneus

Jesus, son of Gmaliel

Mattathias, son of
  Theophilus

Phinehas, son of Samuel

Notes

1. Dallas Willard, *Renewing the Christian Mind: Essays, Interviews, and Talks* (Nashville, TN: HarperCollins, 2016), 304–305.

2. J. Warner Wallace, "Are Young People Really Leaving Christianity?" January 29, 2018, http://coldcasechristianity.com/2018/are-young-people-really-leaving-christianity. Accessed April 15, 2018.

3. Scot McKnight, *The King Jesus Gospel: The Original Good News Revisted* (Grand Rapids, MI: Zondervan, 2011), 20.

4. Barna Group, "Evangelism Is Most Effective Among Kids," October 11, 2004, https://www.barna.com/research/evangelism-is-most-effective-among-kids/

5. *Apostles' Creed: Traditional and Ecumenical Versions* [Online], http://www.umc.org/what-we-believe/apostles-creed-traditional-ecumenical. Accessed April 20, 2018.

6. Old Nicene Creed [Online]. "In glory" and "His kingdom will have no end" were added later at the first Council of Constantinople in 381, http://www.aboutcatholics.com/beliefs/. Accessed April 20, 2018.

7. N. T. Wright, *How God Became King: The Forgotten Story of the Gospels* (New York: Harper Collins, 2012), 41.

8. N. T. Wright, *Luke for Everyone* (Louisville, KY: Westminister John Knox, 2004).

9. N. T. Wright, *The Day the Revolution Began: Reconsidering the Meaning of Jesus' Crucifixion* (New York: Harper Collins, 2016), 72.

10. The idea of leaving this world to go to another world with Christ originated in Greek philosophy, particularly with Plato, who believed the body was a prison cell that held the soul. Our job as humans was to find a way to free our souls to reach the great oversoul. He viewed everything physical as bad, including the body.

11. McKnight, *The King Jesus Gospel*, 36.

12. Talmud, Sukkah 51b; Bava' bathra' 4, https://www.sefaria.org/Sukkah.51b?lang=bi.

13. D. T. Lancaster, *What Is the Kingdom of God?* First Fruits of Zion, audio, http://www.ffoz.org. Lancaster expounds what the Messianic age meant for the Jewish people in his lecture on the concept.

14. B. T. Arnold and B. E. Beyer, *Encountering the Old Testament: A Christian Survey* (Grand Rapids, MI: Baker, 1999), 114.

15. "Ten Plagues for Ten Egyptian Gods and Goddesses," http://www.stat.rice.edu/~dobelman/Dinotech/10_Eqyptian_gods_10_Plagues.pdf.

16. Immediately after leaving Egypt, Moses identifies three groups that are present at the wedding ceremony, mirroring Jesus' three relationships while on Earth. Moses designates three men: Aaron, Nadab, and Abihu, twelve tribes, and seventy elders in Exodus 24. Jesus has an inner circle of three disciples: Peter, James, and John, twelve disciples, and seventy disciples he sends out in Luke 10.

17. Walter C. Kaiser, "Exodus," in *The Expositor's Bible Commentary*, vol. 2, ed. Frank E. Gaebelein (Grand Rapids, MI: Zondervan, 1990), 81–82.

18. Dwight Pryor, *Unveiling the Kingdom* (Dayton, OH: Center for Judaic Studies, 2008), 25.

19. Kaufmann Kohler, "The Kingdom of God," Jewish Encyclopedia, http://www.jewishencyclopedia.com/articles/9328-kingdom-of-god.

20. A harmony of the Gospels chronologically outlines the life of Jesus.

21. D. T. Lancaster, *Depths of Torah* (Marshfield, MO: First Fruits of Zion, 2017), A10.

22. A. B. Simpson, *Christ in the Tabernacle: An Old Testament Portrayal of the Christ of the New Testament* (Camp Hill, PA: Wing Spread, 2009), 7.

23. Roger Liebi, *The Messiah and the Temple: The Symbolism and the Significance of the Second Temple in Light of the New Testament* (Bielefeld, Germany: CMV Press, 2012), 69.

24. When Ezra built the second Temple in 535 BC, he brought all the items taken to Babylon back with him except the ark of the covenant. It is not mentioned in the list in Ezra 1:7–11. First-century historian Josephus and the Mishnah report the disappearance of the ark after the return from Babylon. See Heinrich Andreas C. Hävernick, *A General Historico-Critical Introduction to the Old Testament* (Edingburgh, Scotland: T&T Clark, 1852).

25. Macrobius, Saturnalia, 2:4:11, http://penelope.uchicago.edu/Thayer/l/roman/texts/Macrobius/Saturnalia/2*.html.

26. Max Anders, *Brave New Discipleship: Cultivating Scripture-Driven Christians in a Culture-Driven World* (Nashville, TN: Thomas Nelson, 2015), 189.

27. Josephus, *Antiquities of the Jews*, 11.8.5, http://www.sacred-texts.com/jud/josephus/ant-10.htm.

28. John Anderson, "Daniel: Prophet or Historian?" *Vision*, Winter 2005, http://www.vision.org/visionmedia/religion-and-spirituality-daniel-prophet-historian/1167.aspx. Skeptics have tried to discount that Daniel predated Alexander by 250 years by suggesting the book was written after he died. Anderson dismisses this argument by stating, "The idea is discredited by a statement from Jewish historian Flavius Josephus, writing in the first century C.E. to a Roman audience. Josephus relates an account of the Jewish high priest showing Alexander 'the book of Daniel . . . wherein Daniel declared that one of the Greeks should destroy the empire of the Persians' (*Antiquities of the Jews* 11.8.5)".

29. Travis D. Trost, *Who Should Be King in Israel? A Study of Roman Imperial Politics, the Dead Sea Scrolls, and the Fourth Gospel* (New York, NY: Peter Lang, 2010), 165.

30. Tom Wright, *The Original Jesus: The Life and Vision of a Revolutionary* (Grand Rapids, MI: Eerdmans, 1997), Kindle Locations 646–660.

31. Liebi, *The Messiah and the Temple*, 79.

32. R. Johanan Torta wrote, "Why was the first building [Temple] of Jerusalem destroyed? Because there was in it idol-worship and prohibited relations and the shedding of blood. But in the latter [Temple] we know that they toiled in Torah and were careful with tithes, [so] why were they exiled? Because they love money and each other hates his neighbors." See David Kraemer, *Responses to Suffering in Classical Rabbinic Literature* (New York, NY: Oxford University Press, 1995), 74.

33. Tom Jones and Steve Brown, *The Kingdom of God*, vol. 1 (Spring Hill, TN: DPI Books, 2010), 33.

34. Lois Tverberg, *Reading the Bible with Rabbi Jesus: How a Jewish Perspective Can Transform Your Understanding* (Grand Rapids, MI: Baker, 2018), 31.

35. I expound this concept in chapter 5 of *The Forgotten Jesus*.

36. Dwight A. Pryor, *Unveiling the Kingdom of Heaven* (Dayton, OH: Center for Judaic-Christian Studies; 1st edition, 2008).

37. James Burton Coffman, "Commentary on Micah 2:12," *Coffman Commentaries on the Old and New Testament* (Ablene, TX: Abilene Christian University Press, 1983–1999), https://www.studylight.org/commentaries/bcc/micah-2.html#12.

38. Cyrus Ingerson Scofield, *The Scofield Bible Commentary*, http://www.sacred-texts.com/bib/cmt/sco/mat004.htm.

39. In his book *Hebrew Thought Compared with Greek*, Thorleif Boman writes: "Greek mental activity appears harmonious, prudent, moderate and peaceful; to the person to whom the Greek kind of thinking occurs plainly as ideal, Hebrew thinking and its manner of expression appear exaggerated, immoderate, discordant, and in bad taste.

40. Pryor, *Unveiling the Kingdom of Heaven*.

41. George Eldon Ladd, *A Theology of the New Testament* (Grand Rapids, MI: Eerdmans, 1990), 70.

42. Pryor, *Unveiling the Kingdom of Heaven*.

43. D. T. Lancaster, *Shadows of the Messiah* (Marshfield, MO: First Fruits of Zion, 2005), 161.

44. Clarence Larkin, "The Kingdom," in *Dispensational Truth* (Philadelphia, PA: Twenty-Sixth Publishing, 1918).

45. Tverberg, *Reading the Bible with Rabbi Jesus*, 30.

46. G. K. Beale and Mitchell Kim, *God Dwells Among Us: Expanding Eden to the Ends of the Earth* (Downers Grove, IL: IVP, 2014), 95.

47. Ibid., 96–97.

48. This is the title of N. T. Wright's book.

49. Beale and Kim, *God Dwells Among Us*, 86.

50. Malcolm Muggeridge, *Jesus: The Man Who Lives* (London: Collins, 1975), 61.

51. D. A. Carson, *The Gospel According to John* (Grand Rapids, MI: Eerdmans, 1991), 256.

52. See Num. 19:17–19; Isa. 4:4, 32:15, 44:3, 55:1; Joel 2:28-29, Zech. 13:1.

53. Dallas Willard, *The Divine Conspiracy: Rediscovering Our Hidden Life in God* (New York: HarperCollins, 2009), 19–20.

54. R. Kent Hughes, *Mark: Jesus, Servant and Savior* (Westchester, IL: Crossway, 1989), 33–34.

55. C. S. Song, *Jesus and the Reign of God* (Minneapolis, MN: Fortress, 1993), Kindle Edition: 349–52.

56. Pryor, *Unveiling the Kingdom*.

57. See Shirley Lucass, *The Concept of the Messiah in the Scriptures of Judaism and Christianity* (New York: T&T Clark International, 2011).

58. Ray Vander Laan, "Gates of Hell," https://www.thatthe worldmayknow.com/gates-of-hell-article.

59. Bais Yechiel, *Illuminations: Talmudic Insights into the Chumash* (Jerusalem: Feldheim Publishers, 2006), xvi.

60. G. Campbell Morgan, *The Gospel According to Matthew* (Eugene, OR: Wipf and Stock Publishers, 1929), 215.

61. I believe the number is 70 instead of 72 because of the repeated use of 70 in the Old Testament, particularly in reference to the elders at Sinai in Exodus 24. Moreover, it is an allusion to the table of nations in Genesis 10 as a picture of the movement of Christ extending beyond the Twelve, a picture of the nation of Israel, to the entire world.

62. Willard, *The Divine Conspiracy*, 28.

63. Yechiel Tzvi Lichtenstein, *Commentary on the New Testament: The Holy Gospel According to Mattai* (Marshfield, MO: Vine of David, 2010), on Matthew 2:23.

64. Ray Vander Laan used this term at a Bible conference in Baton Rouge in 2007. He used this label to give a picture of the climate of the first century.

65. Ann Spangler and Lois Tverberg, *Sitting at the Feet of Rabbi Jesus: How the Jewishness of Jesus Can Transform Your Faith* (Grand Rapids, MI: Zondervan, 2009), 44.

66. The technique of connecting two different Scriptures with the same key phrase or word is called *gezera shava* as noted in T. Sanh. 7.11; Abot R. Nat. 37. Both texts utilize the same key word. Steven Notley first documented the Isaiah connection. See R. Steven Notley, "Jesus' Jewish Hermeneutical Method in the Nazareth Synagogue," in *Early Christian Literature and Intertextuality*, vol. 2: Exegetical Studies, ed. C. A. Evans and H. D. Zacharias (London: T&T Clark, 2009), 56.

67. Pryor, *Unveiling the Kingdom of Heaven*.

68. I heard about this concept in Jones and Brown, *The Kingdom of God*, vol. 1, 46.

69. Reggie McNeal, *Kingdom Come: Why We Must Give Up Our Obsession with Fixing the Church—and What We Should Do Instead* (Carol Stream, IL: Tyndale, 2015), 22.

70. Richard B. Hays, *Echoes of Scripture in the Gospels* (Waco, TX: Baylor University Press, 2016), 38.

71. Krister Stendahl in *Christ's Lordship and Religious Pluralism*, ed. Gerald H. Anderson and Thomas F. Stransky (Maryknoll, NY: Orbis, 1981), 233.

72. James Montgomery Boice, *The Gospel of Matthew*, vol. 1 (Grand Rapids, MI: Baker, 2006), 234.

73. Jones and Brown, *The Kingdom of God*, vol. 1, 41.

74. Sinclair Ferguson, *Sermon on the Mount* (Edinburgh: Banner of Truth, 1996), 5.

75. Spangler and Tverberg, *Sitting at the Feet of Rabbi Jesus*, 116.

76. Wilhelm Gesenius and Samuel Prideaux Tregelles, *Gesenius' Hebrew and Chaldee Lexicon to the Old Testament Scriptures* (Bellingham, WA: Logos Bible Software, 2003), 115–16.

77. Tverberg, *Studying the Bible with Rabbi Jesus*, 41.

78. Ibid., 42.

79. David Zaslow, *Reimagining Exodus: A Story of Freedom* (Orleans, MA: Paraclete, 2017), 81.

80. Howard Schwartz, *Reimagining the Bible: The Storytelling of the Rabbis* (New York: Oxford University Press, 1998), 87.

81. Wright, *The Day the Revolution Began*, 162.

82. Midwestern Baptist Theological Seminary New Testament professor Andreas Köstenberger's writing was critical in helping me see this.

83. John G. Stackhouse Jr., *Making the Best of It: Following Christ in the Real World* (New York: Oxford University Press, 2008), 21.

84. McNeal, *Kingdom Come*, 33.

85. John Hutchinson, *Exposition of Paul's Epistle to the Philippians* (Lafayette, IN: Sovereign Grace Publishers, 2001), 214.

86. Some have used this verse to suggest that the church replaced Israel. David Stern in his commentary on the New Testament refutes that idea: "Christians are indeed a chosen people, priests for the King, a holy 'nation' (in a metaphorical sense), a people set aside for God to possess—not by way of superseding the Jews as God's people, but by way of being joined to them by faith in the same God and in the Jewish Messiah. A so-called 'Christian' who opposes or looks down on the Jews as merely God's 'former' people has missed the point altogether." See David H. Stern, *Jewish New Testament Commentary: A Companion Volume to the Jewish New Testament* (Clarksville, MD: Jewish New Testament Publications, 1996).

87. Wright, *The Day the Revolution Began*, 159.

88. Karen H. Jobes, *1 Peter*, Baker Exegetical Commentary on the New Testament (Grand Rapids, MI: Baker Academic, 2005), 161.

89. Jones and Brown, *The Kingdom of God*, vol. 1, 83.

90. Oskar Skarsaune, *In the Shadow of the Temple: Jewish Influences on Early Christianity* (Downers Grove, IL: IVP, 2008), 162.

91. This idea is unpacked in McNeal, *Kingdom Come*, 93.

92. For an in depth study of this text, see Dwight Pryor, "In Whose Image," http://www.jcstudies.org [Audio].

93. Shemuel Safrai, *The Jewish People in the First Century* (Philadelphia, PA: Fortress Press, 1987), 1093.

94. Warren Weirsbe, *The Weirsbe Bible Commentary, New Testament* (Colorado Springs, CO: David C. Cook, 2007), 123.

95. Hate doesn't carry the same meaning today as it did in the first century. The word meant to "love less," expecting loyalty to Jesus superior than any other in one's life.

96. W. K. Volkmer, *These Things: A Reference Manual for Discipleship* (San Antonio, TX: The Passionate Few, 2016), 88.

97. Beale and Kim, *God Dwells Among Us*, 33.

98. John Calvin, *Golden Booklet of the True Christian Life*, trans. Henry J. Van Andel (Grand Rapids, MI: Baker, 1977), 28.

99. Willard, *The Divine Conspiracy*, 22.

100. Dwight Pryor, *Law and Prophets*, http://www.jcstudies.org [Audio].

101. John Phillips, *Exploring the Gospel of Matthew* (Grand Rapids, MI: Kregel, 1999), 94.

102. Kent Hughes, *Sermon on the Mount* (Wheaton, IL: Crossway, 2001), 98.

103. For an in-depth study of this topic see *The Forgotten Jesus*, chapter 2.

104. John Barclay, *Paul and the Gift* (Grand Rapids, MI: Eerdmans, 1997).

105. Ibid., Kindle Locations 473–74.

106. Adrian Rogers, *What Every Christian Ought to Know Day by Day: Essential Truths for Growing Your Faith* (Nashville, TN: B&H Publishing Group, 2008), 70.

107. Robert Lindsey, "The Kingdom of God: God's Power Among Believers," Jerusalem Perspective, January 1, 1990, https://www.jerusalemperspective.com/2445.

108. Jewish Talmud, Makkot 23b–24a, http://sefaria.org/Makkot.23b?lang=bi.

109. Richard M. Davidson, *Flame of Yahweh: Sexuality in the Old Testament* (Peabody, MA: Hendrickson, 2007), 47–48.

110. Beale and Kim, *God Dwells Among Us*, 16.

111. James Hamilton Jr., *God's Indwelling Presence: The Holy Spirit in the Old and New Testaments* (Nashville, TN: B&H, 2006), Kindle Location 779.

112. Lindsey, "The Kingdom of God: God's Power Among Believers."

113. In Avot 3:5, Rabbi Nehunya describes the pull of the "yoke of mundane matters" on those who have set aside "the yoke of Torah." God provides for the needs of those who have submitted themselves under the yoke of the Torah. See Joseph Frankovic, "Where Seed and Thistle Grow," Jersalem Perspective, July 1, 2007, https://www.jerusalemperspective.com/4683.

114. Ferguson, *Sermon on the Mount*, 3.

115. Dietrich Bonhoeffer, *Life Together: The Classic Exploration of Christian in Community* (New York, NY: HarperOne, 2009), 111.

116. Warren W. Wiersbe, *5 Secrets of Living* (Wheaton, IL: Tyndale House, 1977), 79.

117. Mark Dever, "The Certain Victory of Christ's Church as Encouragement to Evangelism," Together for the Gospel, March 2014, http://t4g.org/media/2014/03/the-certain-victory-of-christs-church-an-encouragement-to-evangelism/.

118. I devoted two chapters in my book *Firmly Planted* defusing this argument.

119. Frankovic, "Where the Seed and Thistle Grow," www.jerusalemperspective.com/4683.

120. Bill Hull and Ben Sobels, *The Discipleship Gospel Primer* (Nashville, TN: Discipleship.Org Publishing, 2017), Kindle Location 129.

121. Willard, *Renewing the Christian Mind*, 304.

122. Ferguson, *Sermon on the Mount*, 77.

123. Beale and Kim, *God Dwells Among Us*, 114.

124. Willard, *Renewing the Christian Mind*, 274.

125. C. S. Lewis, *Mere Christianity* (New York: Macmillan, 1956), 148.

126. Dietrich Bonhoeffer, *The Cost of Discipleship* (London: MacMillan, 1968), 67.

127. Herman Bavinck, *Our Reasonable Faith* (Grand Rapids, MI: Eerdmans, 1956), 475.

128. Robby Gallaty, *Bearing Fruit: What Happens When God's People Grow* (Nashville, TN: B&H Publishing Group, 2017), 5.

129. Dallas Willard, "Live Life to the Full," Christian Herald, April 14, 2001, http://www.dwillard.org/articles/artview.asp?artID=5.

130. Martin Luther, "A Mighty Fortress Is Our God," published 1531.

131. John Piper, *Future Grace: The Purifying Power of the Promises of God* (Colorado Springs, CO: Multnomah, 1998).

132. Donald Whitney, *Spiritual Disciplines for the Christian Life* (Colorado Springs, CO: Navpress, 1997), 21.

133. Adrian Rogers, "7 Reasons Why a Saved Person Can't Be Lost" https://www.oneplace.com/ministries/love-worth-finding /read/articles/7-reasons-why-a-saved-person-cant-be-lost-8545.html.

134. Hamilton, *God's Indwelling Presence,* Kindle Location 3448.

135. Beale and Kim, *God Dwells Among Us,* 36.

136. Alan Kreider, *The Change of Coversion and the Origin of Cristendom* (Eugene, OR: Wipf and Stock, 1999), 14.

137. Ibid., 20.

138. Krister Stendahl, *Meanings: The Bible as Document and as Guide,* 2nd. ed. (Minneapolis, MN: Fortress, 2008), 236.

139. John Dickson, *The Best Kept Secret of Christian Mission: Promoting the Gospel with More Than Our Lips* (Grand Rapids, MI: Zondervan, 2010), Kindle Locations 203–205.

140. A gospel presentation should always be followed by an invitation to follow Christ, or it's not a biblical evangelistic invitation.

141. McKnight, *The King Jesus Gospel,* Kindle Location 480.

142. Ibid., 1279.

143. Willard, *The Divine Conspiracy,* 38.

144. Ibid., 57–58.

145. Ibid.

146. Beale and Kim, *God Dwells Among Us,* 13.

147. "Sold! One Declaration of Independence Copy," NBC News, March 23, 2007, http://www.nbcnews.com/id/17761718/ns/us_news-life/t/sold-one-declaration-independence-copy/#.Wtdjcy7wzhE.

148. Charles L. Quarles, *Sermon on the Mount,* NAC Studies in Bible and Theology (Nashville, TN: B&H Publishing Group, 2011), 11.

149. Willard, *The Divine Conspiracy,* 105.

150. Arnold Fruchtenbaum, *Yeshua: The Life of Messiah from a Messianic Jewish Perspective* (San Antonio, TX: Ariel Ministries, 2016), 287.

151. D. T. Lancaster, *The Holy Epistle to the Galatians* (Marshfield, OH: First Fruits of Zion, 2011), 180.

152. Ibid.

153. Jonathan Pennington, *The Sermon on the Mount and Human Flourishing: A Theological Commentary* (Grand Rapids, MI: Baker, 2017), 177.

154. Ibid., 78.

155. D. T. Lancaster, *Chronicles of the Messiah*, 475.

156. Fruchtenbaum, *Yeshua*, 273.

157. Pennington, *The Sermon on the Mount*, 42. According to Pennington, this word is connected to the Greek word *asre*, which "describes a happy state of the one who lives wisely . . . [and] refers to true happiness and flourishing within the gracious covenant God has given." Ibid., 44.

158. Ibid., 43

159. Ellen Charry, *God and the Art of Happiness* (Grand Rapids: Eerdmans, 2010), 170.

160. R. T. France, *Gospel of Matthew* (Grand Rapids, MI: Eerdmans, 2007), 160.

161. Alfred Edersheim, *The Life and Times of Jesus the Messiah,* 3rd ed. (Grand Rapids, MI: Eerdmans, 1953), 528–29.

162. Eugene Peterson, *Eat This Book: A Conversation in the Art of Spiritual Reading* (Grand Rapids: Eerdmans, 2009), 43–44.

163. R. T. France, *Gospel of Matthew*, 161. Someone said that the Beatitudes stand at the beginning of the message like the Ten Commandments stand at the beginning of the Mosaic Law. See H. Benedict Green, *Matthew, Poet of Beatitudes* (Edinburg; T&T Clark, 2001), 284.

164. Martyn Lloyd-Jones, *Studies in Sermons on the Mount*, vol. 1 (Grand Rapids, MI: Eerdmans, 1973), 69.

165. Ferguson, *Sermon on the Mount*, 69, 71.

166. Green, *Matthew, Poet of Beatitudes*, 288.

167. Lancaster, *Chronicles of Messiah*, 466.

168. Phillips, *Exploring the Gospel of Matthew*, 94.

169. France, *The Gospel of Matthew*, 183.

170. Douglas Moo, "The Law of Moses or the Law of Christ," in *Continuity and Discontinuity: Perspectives on the Relationship Between the Old and New Testaments: Essays in Honor of S. Lewis Johnson Jr.*, ed. J. S. Feinberg (Westchester, IL: Crossway, 1988), 203–18.

171. John MacArthur, *Matthew 1–7* (Chicago, IL: Moody, 1985), 303.

172. John Owen, *The Works of John Owen*, ed. William H. Goold, 24 vols. (Edinburgh: Johnstone & Hunter, 1850–1855; reprint by Banner of Truth Trust, 1965, 1991), 6:9.

173. Quarles, *Sermon on the Mount*, 171.

174. Ferguson, *Sermon on the Mount*, 114.

175. Pryor, *Unveiling the Kingdom of Heaven*.

176. Ibid.

177. Pennington, *Sermon on the Mount*, 249.

178. Willard, "Live Life to the Full," http://www.dwillard.org/articles/artview.asp?artID=5.

179. See Matthew W. Bates, *Salvation by Allegiance Alone: Rethinking Faith, Works, and the Gospel of King Jesus* (Grand Rapids, MI: Baker). Although I don't agree with everything in the book, I was challenged to think about faith as allegiance and not just agreeing to intellectual facts.

180. Quarles, *Sermon on Mount*, 299.

181. Craig Keener, *Gospel of Matthew* (Grand Rapids, MI: Eerdmans, 2009), 245.

182. Quarles, *Sermon on the Mount*, 333.

183. Dwight Pryor revealed this concept to me at a Haverim Study in April 2007 in Dayton, Ohio.

184. Lancaster, *Chronicles of Messiah*, 476.

185. Tim Keller, foreword to *The Whole of Christ: Legalism, Antinomianism and Gospel Assurance—Why the Marrow Controversy Still Matters*, by Sinclair B. Ferguson (Wheaton, IL: Crossway, 2016), 16.

186. Eugene Boring, Klaus Berger, and Carsten Colpe, *Hellenistic Commentary to the New Testament* (Nashville, TN: Abingdon, 1995), 202.

187. Darrell Bock, *Jesus According to Scripture: Restoring the Portrait from the Gospels* (Grand Rapids, MI: Baker, 2002), 152–53.

188. Stanley Hauweras, *Resident Aliens* (Nashville, TN: Abingdon, 1989), 74.

Disciplemaking resources to grow your people.

"An outstanding introduction to the basics of the faith in a manner that will equip Christians to grow into maturity."

THOM S. RAINER

"I want to encourage you as clearly as I possibly can. Please don't read this book. Instead, do it."

DAVID PLATT

"Read this book, be encouraged, and then pass it on to a fellow pilgrim."

RUSSELL D. MOORE